ARE ALL CHRISTIANS MINISTERS?

JOHN N. COLLINS completed postgraduate studies in the Bible on the eve of the Second Vatican Council at the Pontifical Bibical Institute in Rome and at the Ecole Biblique in Jerusalem.

In 1971 he returned to bible studies at the University of London King's College where he researched the origins of the Christian concept of ministry. This doctoral work attracted two awards for further research during 1976-77 at the Ecumenical Institute in Tantur, Israel.

His pathfinding work, which includes a comprehensive critique of contemporary trends in the theology of ministry, was published in 1990 under the title *Diakonia: Re-interpreting the Ancient Sources.*

The same year he wrote the present study during a fellowship from the Ecumenical Institute, Collegeville, Minnesota, on sabbatical release from high school teaching in Melbourne, where he lives with his wife and two middle teenagers, close by the beaches of Seaford.

ARE ALL CHRISTIANS MINISTERS?

JOHN N. COLLINS

A Liturgical Press Book

 THE LITURGICAL PRESS
Collegeville, Minnesota

To my brothers and sisters
Geoff, Joan, Barbara, Jennifer, Michael
and to
Mary, Barry, Alan, Judy
sisters and brothers too

Published in North America in 1992 by
The Liturgical Press
St John's Abbey,
Collegeville, MN 56321-7500

Originally published in Australia by
E. J. Dwyer (Australia) Pty Ltd / David Lovell Publishing

Library of Congress Cataloging-in-Publication Data
Collins, John N. (John Neil), 1931–
    Are all Christians ministers? / John N. Collins
      p. cm.
    Includes bibliographical references.
    ISBN 0-8146-2168-6
    1. Church work—Catholic Church. 2. Pastoral theology —Catholic
Church. 3. Lay ministry—Catholic Church. 4. Pastoral theology—
History. I. Title.
BX2347.0655 1992
253—dc20   92-9599
                                                CIP

Cover design and illustration by Stanley Wong
Designed by David Lovell
Typeset in 10½/12pt Baskerville by ACP Colour Graphics, Sydney.
Printed in Singapore by Fong & Sons Printers Pte Ltd

Preface

This book claims that we must rethink and remake ministry in our churches. It takes up and advances the argument of its scholarly predecessor *Diakonia: Re-interpreting the Ancient Sources* (New York: Oxford University Press, 1990).

The book aims to familiarize readers with how the first Christians viewed ministry, and theologians in particular may wish to be advised that it makes some advances on positions taken in the earlier study. Two of these are in clarifying the nature of the ministry of the Seven in Acts 6 and in disentangling ministry and charisma at 1 Corinthians 12.

With some experience of how slowly theology takes new ideas on board and with some perception of how hesitantly institutions adopt ideas which might affect their view of themselves, I have sought to reach especially those Christians who are not theologians yet wish to deepen their appreciation of ministry. My hope is that from the desire for renewal and indeed from the clamour of such people renewal in ministry might quicken sooner than is likely through mere theological debate and ecclesiastical positionings.

The book was written in the course of a fellowship during the fall semester of 1990 at the Institute for Ecumenical and Cultural Research, Collegeville, Minnesota. In preparing the manuscript for publication during the Christmas vacation at home in Melbourne a year later, I wrote a new introductory chapter. To Kilian P. McDonnell, OSB, president of the institute, Patrick G. Henry, its director, and to the institute's board I am deeply indebted for a rare opportunity of enjoying both the time and the appropriate facilities for writing. The writing was done on a laptop computer considerably made available by Liam G. Davison, principal of John Paul College, Frankston, the high school where I teach; with the college's business manager, Kevin La Fontaine, he also facilitated other arrangements affecting my leave. I also record my appreciation of the interest shown in my study tour and of support for it by Sir Frank Little, Archbishop of Melbourne.

To other staff associated with the institute at Collegeville, Dolores Schuh, CHM, and Wilfred Theisen, OSB, our family of four say again a warm thank you for a myriad of kindnesses in the course of our first experience of winter in the land of Lake Wobegon. Our renewed thanks also to fellow residents of the institute during our semester there for the warmth and laughter of friendships so quickly made and so long to be treasured.

J. N. C.
Seaford
6 January 1992

> '*the whole people of God are called to be involved in ministry...*'
> '*it is not a biblical point of view that ministry in the church is restricted only to ordained ministers...*'
> '*The call to the ministry ... applies to all of God's people...*'
> '*Baptism is a sign of gifts for ministry for all people...*'
> '*The church as a whole is called into the ministry of reconciliation...*'

This then is a truly representative Protestant point of view for our time and makes no bones about where Protestants currently like to locate ministry in the church. Would official Roman Catholic theology be just as happy with this? Of course not, although the Vatican response to this aspect of *BEM*'s theology is discreet in expressing its reservations. Less so are the responses of the Orthodox churches which speak of '*ambiguous formulation*' and '*equivocation*' creating confusion between the roles of hierarchy and people. Anyone can appreciate this kind of reaction from such ancient churches with such a clear demarcation between their ministerial ranks and the rest of the baptized.

Where one church (the United Protestant Church of Belgium) acknowledges in its response the potential for conflicting interpretations at this point of *BEM* and speaks of 'an almost unbearable tension' in the document 'between ministry and community', the response from the Church of England prefers to see in *BEM*'s formulations—perhaps to no one's surprise—a successful compromise which holds together 'two hitherto apparently contrasting views'.

The response from our own study, by contrast, will be uncompromising on this issue. In confiding exclusive rights to ministry to those who are officially commissioned to ministry within their churches, however, our study will not merely be playing into the hands of a committee of Roman Catholic or Orthodox theologians and churchmen. Clearly, to argue and to attempt to illustrate from the earliest Christian tradition, as we shall do, that authentic Christian ministry can only really be a restricted role within a church is seemingly to bolster the so-called conservative or hierarchical theologies of ministry. But at one significant point

1: The Shapes of Ministry Today

Are all Christians ministers?

'No,' say these chapters.

This blunt claim will surprise more Christians than it will please. If, nonetheless, it prompts them to pursue the reason for the claim in the following chapters, some good will have been done for the notion of church and for the place of ministry within it in our time.

Those whom the blunt answer pleases, on the other hand, will also do well to consider what follows because, more likely than not, their present convictions about who are ministers in the church prevent them from considering whether others in the church might also rightfully and usefully be known as ministers.

Who are those for whom all Christians are ministers? In the first place they are members of those numerous Protestant churches which publicly maintain that all members are ministers. This belief is sometimes spelt out in a reframed modern constitution. More generally, in these churches' official responses to the Lima statement on ministry (*Baptism, Eucharist and Ministry*, known as *BEM*, and drawn up after protracted international consultations under the auspices of the Faith and Order Commission of the World Council of Churches and published in Geneva in 1982), church leaders, delegates and prominent theologians have consistently hailed the adoption of the idea in *BEM* that ministry is a capacity with which each member of a church is endowed.

Thus, leafing through the six volumes of *Churches respond to BEM (1986-1988)*, we constantly encounter appreciative commendations of this point of departure for the statement's theology of ministry. These occur in phrases about *'the whole people of God and their ministry'*, and the following are some more of them; their central idea is worth emphasising from the start (hence more italics):

CONTENTS

at least our study will diverge as decisively from the current Roman and Orthodox hierarchical models as I have already indicated it must do from the major Protestant consensus. And this is at the point where women come into consideration. Against official Roman and Orthodox pronouncements and regulations to the contrary, our study lays bare the ground on which, according to the mind of the first Christian men and women, ministry is as connatural to women as the churches have traditionally claimed it is to men.

These two issues, then, the availability of women for ministry and the unavailability of ministry to all, are two serious and disputed issues in our contemporary churches which our study will be relevant to. Other ministerial issues will be incidental to these; they might be the interchange of ministry between churches, the permanency of ministry, initiation into ministry, and so on. But first we should explore the reason for yet another book about ministry and its significance for the kind of church we believe we have inherited from our traditions.

Crisis centre

The books and studies about ministry which have proliferated over the last twenty years are themselves evidence of a felt need for constant review of what ministry means to the churches. In their diversity and sometimes in their passion these studies further evidence a sense across almost all churches that something substantial is unresolved about ministry and that the churches are hurting. Talk of crisis is standard, and the word 'crisis' regularly features in titles of books and papers.

In its response to *BEM* in 1988 the Federation of the Evangelical Churches of what was then the German Democratic Republic went so far as to say that 'the crisis in which the ordained ministry finds itself today in the world and in the church ... is an indispensable part of every discussion on the ministry.' (*Churches respond*, vol. 5, p. 146) If we reflect that this is the measured judgement of thoroughly informed leaders of over seven million Christians from one coherent region, the observation is alarming. And a further critical aspect of the situation which these leaders point to is that the ordained ministers themselves are suffering from 'a lack of assurance, or a loss of a certainty as to the significance and shape of their ministry.' Making this situation even worse, in their view, is 'a widely observable refusal to acknowledge the reality of this situation' and 'an administrative rigidity' which presumably prevents anyone coming to grips with the problems.

Some readers would be more familiar with this kind of exasperated concern on the part of churchmen and theologians within the Roman Catholic Church. Illustrating this is a notorious attempt during 1991 by the archbishop of Milwaukee, Rembert Weakland, in the face of the growing shortage of priests in his church, to advocate the advancement of married men to ordination; the tentative proposal was summarily dismissed as 'out of place' by Vatican authorities. Only with difficulty can we not see here in the Vatican's response to the statistical crisis of ordained ministers the 'administrative rigidity' which the German Evangelical leaders deplored in their own church.

For over twenty years sociologists like those working through the Pro Mundi Vita International Research and Information Center in Brussels have published analyses of the growing numerical inadequacy of the Roman Catholic clergy. An account of some of this earlier research which is still easily accessible by the general reader is Jan Kerkhofs' 'From Frustration to Liberation?' in *Minister? Pastor? Prophet?* Kerkhofs presented numerous regional profiles like the following: in Latin America over the decade 1965-75 not only had the numbers studying for the priesthood declined by more than 15% but the numbers of those progressing to ordination had also declined from 63% to 44%, and this during a period when the continent's population increased by seventy million. One of his concluding observations, accordingly, relates to the 'tragedy of the church leaders' who felt obliged to accommodate themselves to the 'rigidity and anxiety of a closed' Vatican way of thinking (p. 20) which is locked into 'the fight to the death over the widening of the scope of the ministry' (p. 18).

In the decade and more following heavily publicised assessments of this kind, the Vatican championed the cause of the type of ministry and priesthood it required by similarly publicising figures from its Central Office for Church Statistics showing an increase in students for the priesthood from some 63,000 in 1978 to some 93,500 in 1989, leaving the public with the impression, as Vatican watcher Peter Hebblethwaite had put it earlier, that 'the church has weathered the vocations crisis.' (*National Catholic Reporter*, 9 November 1990). The figures are of little meaning for a reduction of the crisis, however, when we do not know whether the proportion proceeding to ordination has similarly increased. We must also take into account that the greatest increases are in developing countries where cultural and economic factors other than ministerial aspirations affect enrolments.

Archbishop Pio Laghi, who as secretary of the Vatican's Congregation for Catholic Education, had responsibility for the development of education in ministry, clearly signaled that such numbers were not enough when he identified the three factors working against them; these were the ongoing deaths of the increasingly ageing incumbent clergy, the continuing 'defections' of ministers in the field, and the irreversible and mounting disproportion between numbers of ordained ministers and rampantly ballooning populations (*L'Osservatore Romano*, 29 October 1990). To counter this crisis a Vatican committee subsequently produced a proposal almost Gilbertian in its grotesqueness. It involved shifting clergy from clergy-rich regions to clergy-deprived regions: shifting them, as the report put it, 'from one pole to another' (*Origins*, 28 March 1991). This concept was endorsed by Pope John Paul II in his letter to priests on Holy Thursday 1991 (printed in the same issue of *Origins*). In the meantime the central telling statistics stood in 1991 as Archbishop Laghi put them: 73% of all ordained ministers in the Roman Catholic Church reside in Europe and the United States servicing the needs of merely 38% of the planet's Roman Catholic Christians. Even then, of the 174 ordained priests of the church of Seattle in 1989 only 94 are projected to be in service by the year 2000.

Epicentre

But that is merely the statistical drama. The much more dramatic question, beyond statistics, is the one singled out by the German Evangelical leaders cited above, and this concerns the ordained minister's sense of identity and assurance. Within the Roman Catholic Church the concern has long been particularly acute, as we shall see, although Vatican response to the multifarious evidence supporting this assessment has been no more enlightened than its response to the critical shortfall of priests. These two crises are, of course, intimately related.

Pope John Paul II, whose empathy with his priestly confreres is one of his most marked characteristics, has assiduously sought to uphold and enhance a paradigm of priesthood which he brought to the papacy from Eastern Europe. The Holy Thursday letter to priests just alluded to succinctly outlines the paradigm and anticipates what John Paul proposes in the Apostolic Exhortation, *Pastores Dabo Vobis* ('I will provide you with pastors'), in response to the Roman synod of October 1990 on the formation of priests. The paradigm's main features bear re-presenting here because in the pope's view the obscuring of these has led to what he too acknowledges to be 'the crisis of priestly identity'.

The most striking feature—for those at least who come to John Paul II's letter familiar with other perceptions of priesthood more frequently presented in contemporary theological literature—is the cultic and sacrificial character of the priesthood upheld by the pope. That is to say, in seeking to identify 'the very essence of the sacramental priesthood', John Paul II presents the priest in a cultic role (*sacerdos* in Latin) rather than as presbyter, which was the original designation both in old English (*preost*) and in the original Greek (the word meaning *elder*) and which the Second Vatican Council once more significantly adopted and powerfully endorsed.

Thus in this document the ordained 'priest' is essentially characterized in the pope's timeworn Roman Catholic Latin phrase *sacerdos alter Christus,* 'the priest is another Christ', and is said to act '*in persona Christi*', another Latin phrase from the classical medieval theology of priesthood translated literally 'in the person of Christ' and most dubiously derived from the Latin Vulgate translation of Paul's phrase at 2 Corinthians 2.10 (a totally different context, with the phrase commonly translated as 'in the presence of Christ'). Lest the cultic and sacrificial dimension of this essentially medieval characterization of the priest be overlooked, John Paul identifies the ordained priest with the high priest of Hebrews 5.1, 'chosen from among men' and 'appointed to act on behalf of men in relation to God'. (The passage draws on imagery and theology derived from the priestly ritual of the Jewish temple and ancient tabernacle.) In accord with this, the ordained priests are 'ministers of the divine mysteries' and recipients of 'the sacred power of the priesthood'. The power relates especially to celebrating the sacrament of the eucharist which Jesus placed 'in the hands of the apostles and, through them, in the hands of the church'. At that moment Jesus initiated an historical succession of sacramental ordination by 'the imposition of hands'. The sacrament of order 'imprints on the soul of the priest a special character which, once it has been received, remains in him as a source of sacramental grace...'. Conscious of this historic procession of the sacrament through the ages, 'through generation after generation of priests' and 'entrusted also to us in the present moment of human and world history', the pope raises this priesthood to a mystic and indeed to an eschatological plane.

This profile is familiar to all whose experience of the Roman Catholic mass reaches back to the 1950s and 1960s when virtually every priest faithfully modelled it and frequently expounded its significations. Theological handbooks of the time expounded nothing else. And today, in the midst of numerous attempts to provide other theological profiles of the Roman Catholic priesthood, some writers have continued to argue the singular importance and uphold the enduring validity of the one described by Pope John Paul II.

Thus in Jean Galot's *Theology of the Priesthood* (1985 in its English translation) we read how 'the priest is a representative of Christ and exercises certain powers in his name' (p. 27); as the Twelve were 'the first recipients of the priesthood' they were assigned 'a mediating position' to enable other Christians to achieve union with Christ (p. 74); 'In today's language, Jesus transmitted to the Twelve his own priesthood....' (p. 77):

> It is important to insist that Jesus willed a succession marked by historical continuity with himself and with the group of the Twelve, for to this group he handed over the totality of priestly power.... [The Holy Spirit] bestows the

priestly power only through a chain of historical transmission in which the Twelve are the first link (p. 87).

The other links for the transmission of power through the ages are forged by ordination by which new priests receive their priestly conformation:

> Through the mark it imprints, ordination fashions a new being (p. 202). ... there emerges from the priestly character the capacity to make the Lord present. If the priest is 'another Christ' in a special way, this is due ... to the figure of Christ Priest and Shepherd impressed in his soul (p. 207).

In his more recent *Priesthood* (1990) Patrick J. Dunn upholds the same understanding of the priest as 'Marked by an indelible character at the time of his ordination' and thereby 'empowered to act "in the person of Christ the Head" ... pre-eminently "in the mystery of the Eucharistic sacrifice"' (p. 170); this role the priest carries out within a church 'instituted and hierarchically structured by Christ himself' (p. 169). Contrary views—and there are many contrary views—arise, in the dire view expressed by Aidan Nichols at the conclusion of his *Holy Order* (1990), under the influence of 'the powers all Christians foreswear in baptism; the world, the flesh and the devil' (p. 143), and they work against the 'high doctrine of the priest, as the living extension of the ministry of the Word Incarnate', which was the theological reading of priesthood in the French school of the seventeenth century (Bérulle, Olier), which profoundly influenced all subsequent thinking about Catholic priesthood until the middle of the twentieth century, and which for Nichols 'has become part and parcel of the patrimony of Latin Catholicism' (p. 115). The ideal here would be that of Chocarne, the nineteenth century biographer of the renowned Lacordaire: 'Its form, of a directly Divine origin, remains ever the same' (*The Inner Life*, p. 70).

From other writers—Greshake, Castellucci, even the staunchly traditional populariser George A. Kelly—we could illustrate the ongoing task some assume of repeating or lightly reworking the theology of priesthood which derives from the medieval and

Tridentine periods. All these writers evidence a lively awareness that over recent decades other theologians have been venturing in directions away from this traditional Roman Catholic line of thought so clearly represented in Pope John Paul II's letter above. Thus Greshake entered the discussion under our own heading, naming his first chapter *Priesthood in crisis* and its first section (taking a phrase from another theologian) *Everything is tottering,* concluding it with the question, 'If everything is tottering, where is the fixed centre of the priest's office which characterizes and supports the holder of that office?' (p. 18).

This last is a strange question, clearly, nearly thirty years after the Dogmatic Constitution on the Church (1964) and the Decree on the Ministry and Life of Priests (1965) in the Second Vatican Council, after a special Roman synod on ministerial priesthood in 1971 (Edward Schillebeeckx provides an informative account of the conflicting views on priesthood debated at this synod in *The Church with a Human Face,* pp. 211-236) and still later synods on the closely related subjects of laity in 1987 and on the formation of priests in 1990. Interestingly one of the earliest writers to treat priestly ministry from the perspective of crisis, Charles E. Curran, eschewed any attempt to find a 'center' in the teaching of the Vatican council, and even in 1972, in *The Crisis in Priestly Ministry,* worked on the principle that there are 'a myriad of possible models of ministry' (p. 30).

Pope John Paul II's evaluation of the council documents is of course very different. For him, as he inferred in the letter we have used, talk of crisis may not have arisen had the conciliar documents been correctly read. Like Curran, however, theologians have sought in vain to abstract from the conciliar and subsequent documents a coherent teaching about priesthood. Avery Dulles found three main interpretations among theologians—priesthood as ministry of the word, as a cultic or sacramental ministry, and as a ministry of leadership—and attributed the diversity to what he called 'the studied ambiguity of Vatican II' ('Models for Ministerial Priesthood', *Origins,* 11 October 1990). Kenan Osborne also emphasizes contradictory elements in the council's presentation of priestly ministry (*Priesthood: A History,* p. 322), while in an address marking twenty years since the closing of the council Archbishop Rembert Weakland drew attention to the 'deficiency' in the council's teaching on ordained priesthood, which remained for him one of the 'unresolved issues ... full of ambiguities'. ('From Dream to Reality to Vision', *Origins* 11, October 1990) Not surprisingly, in considering 'Priestless Parishes: Priests' Perspective' within what it recognised as the contemporary 'ferment in the church with regard to ministers and ministries', the National Federation of Priests' Councils in the United States concluded that 'Definitive work on the theology of orders and priesthood in the Catholic tradition remains to be done.' (*Origins*, 30 May 1991)

From priest to minister

If there is no clarity about what the main push has been for in this disturbed area of the theology of ordained priesthood, we can arrive at some perception of where the push has been coming from. Whereas the older theologies usually began from the idea of Jesus establishing a line of official priests, the newer theology has at last come to terms with the historical problem which such a theory runs up against. The gospels are just not the kind of historical document which can provide a pedigree of priesthood. Accordingly people have turned away from looking for the meaning of the various church ministries in the obscure history of particular offices like those of bishop and priest and have turned instead to the idea of ministry itself.

In the idea of ministry modern writers have undoubtedly picked on one of the central perceptions of the early Christians about the way they were bonded together in church, and we are going to be looking closely at the early Christian idea from chapter 3 onwards. Out of the current understanding of it a conviction has been building that ministry is not something which is a prerogative of the bishop or priest but is a role that each Christian is cast into at baptism. *A Church of the Baptised* is the very title chosen by Rémi Parent for his assault on the problem announced by his subtitle, *Overcoming the Tension between the Clergy and the Laity*; if baptism makes all Christians 'the subject of salvation', it must also thereby make them all 'the subject of ecclesiastical life' (p. 81). Writing from a similar perspective—and a perspective similar to our own—in *Priesthood and Ministry in Crisis,* Terence Card put the view clearly (pp. 119-120):

> Now if neither the language of priestliness nor that of apostleship in the traditional sense are central to the New Testament, what is? It is in fact the language of discipleship. That gospel theme becomes the 'in Christ' of St Paul, emphasising that the context of all ministries is the whole body of the people of God. *All* are called to be in Christ; *all* are endowed with gifts of service for the building up of the Body of Christ; some are called to exercise their particular gifts of leadership as a service in the body of Christ.

In *A Theology of Ministry* Michael Lawler has produced a striking formulation of the same inclusive view of churchwide or 'ecclesial' ministry, to use his word which has attained official currency in this use in the United States (p. 83):

> The ministerial church comes before its ministers and its ecclesial ministers come before its ordained ministers.

To appreciate the force of this new approach to ministry in the church we need to notice that, while the leader in this view of church is indeed a leader, the service or ministry he or she performs is of the same kind as the ministry with which the other Christians are endowed. The leader is just doing something different; the leader is not endowed with a different kind of ministry but with a different 'gift' within the sphere of ministry.

People have been seizing on this idea with the enthusiasm with which one greets a breakthrough. For some it makes redundant the search for a theology of particular offices like those of bishop and priest because those offices are just particular roles within a churchwide ministry. The theology of ministry is all. Such an idea has a mighty power to work for the change of present structures in those churches especially which hold their particular offices in the highest esteem as coming to them from the earliest generations of the church and as carrying with them the authority of the Lord.

We see the two views clash in an interesting statement from Cardinal William Baum made in his then capacity of Prefect of the Congregation for Seminaries and Catholic Institutions in the Vatican. The statement of 28 September 1988 marked the conclusion of a five-year investigation of seminaries in the United States, and the cardinal strongly emphasised the need for the seminaries to uphold in particular an understanding of the priesthood which is (his emphasis) '*sound, theologically informed, in accordance with the teaching of the Magisterium of the church*' ('A Message on the Priesthood', p. 151). Given the cardinal's responsibility for the seminaries, this insistence is understandable and indeed predictable. Our point of interest is that the cardinal proceeded from this position to consider some phenomena within the church of today which threaten to obscure 'the distinctive character of the ordained priesthood', and first among these is, in his words, 'the rather generalised *concept of ministry*' (p. 153. The other phenomena are the renewed emphasis on the common priesthood of all the faithful, crisis of confidence in priestly celibacy, and pressures for the ordination of women).

Many men and especially women are nonetheless impelled to work for change in the ministerial structures by virtue of what they feel the modern notion of ministry, if followed through, could do for the church of today. In particular it could make ministry available on a far broader scale than has ever been considered possible before. At one stroke it could mean the end of male dominated ministry in those churches which still maintain it. And we could hold up to our fellow Christians the brilliant vision of a newly enlivened church which the ministerial people could really make their own. The task for the present, on this view, is to raise the ministerial consciousness of the baptized and to prepare to deploy the ministerial energies once these begin to show.

The energies which this broadbased approach to ministry has already been releasing are immense, just as is the resentment in most quarters at the unwillingness of the larger Christian churches to amend their law or custom to accommodate the surge. There is some ironic justice in the pressure which these ministerially conscious people are putting their church authorities under. They are the vanguard of that people of God whom historically the great church failed to make really part of the church. If it is only since Vatican II that the people have begun to be conscious of themselves as the people of God, they largely retain oppressive memories of when they were merely 'the faithful', so named, I am afraid, less in an awareness of the faith which saves or because they were a people enlivened through their communal experience of encounter with the divine but because they were thereby reminded of their duty to be faithful to the doctrinal formulations of the hierarchy. These people are now in many places a vast resource for making real in life the gospel of reconciliation and freedom, and it is under the banner of ministry that they are being encouraged.

What now for the question in the front of this book?
Are all Christians ministers?
Yes, says the movement for reform.
No, say the following pages.

2: Shapes of Church

In this chapter we will consider what difference it makes for the kind of church we would like to see if we take a broader rather than a narrower view of a church's ministerial capability. In considering this we will take a close look at one biblical passage to see how modern images of church have been affected by changes in the way the passage has been translated. The passage is Ephesians 4.11-12, but before presenting it in its various English translations we will do well to give a little thought to the idea of translation itself. Because our foundational Christian documents were written in Greek—and Greek of a particular period from a variety of authors who each came under varied and complex cultural influences—our churches of the late twentieth century are beholden to the linguists who translate the documents into English and indeed into the nearly two thousand other languages in which biblical literature is now available. What happens in this process of carrying ideas from one language to another?

Some tricks of translating

In translating we seek to represent in our own language the meaning or intention of the foreign writer or speaker. The better translations, as would seem to be obvious, are those which the original writer or speaker would acknowledge as most nearly representing his or her own original intention. To arrive at this intention is the first task of the translator, and that is often challenging in itself. The next step is more challenging and usually very difficult because the intention or meaning of, say, a French fantasy has to be equivalently expressed in, say, English, where structures, sounds, word values and associations are totally different. At exercises in translation the school student will usually slavishly, as the saying is, translate word for word, keeping an eye mainly perhaps on establishing the correct word order. In the meantime all the original fantasy of the French piece will have disappeared.

In his *Semantics of New Testament Greek* J. P. Louw gives the extreme example of the furphy one can end up with by a mechanical word for word process of translation. The familiar sentence 'The spirit is willing but the flesh is weak' was given to a translation machine for rendering into Japanese, and then again for rendering of the Japanese back into English where it ended up as 'There is some good whisky but the roast beef is mediocre' (p. 71).

The same writer provides the following comparison of two translations of a short passage from Paul's letter to Philippians (1.3-5), the first being the *Revised Standard Version* (*RSV*) and the second the *Good News* or *Today's English Version* (*TEV*) (p. 87). In the first the reader will notice that the language is not quite the way we would express ourselves if we were wishing to convey these sentiments, whereas we could probably imagine expressing ourselves in the manner of the second translation. A word of explanation about this. The differences are not accidental but arise from different theories about what makes a translation good and from different opinions about whether in certain circumstances one method of translating might be more appropriate than another. Thus one translator may choose to keep close to what writers in semantics call the surface structure of the original language, following closely its layout and general pattern as well as seeking to put the ideas into English. The second translator, by contrast, like *TEV* below, will totally discard the Greek patterns and concentrate solely on identifying the meaning conveyed by those patterns, and will seek then to use appropriate English patterns to express the meaning. The two versions can be strikingly different, as in the following instances.

RSV: I thank my God in all my remembrance of you, always in every prayer of mine for you all making my prayer with joy, ... thankful for your partnership in the gospel from the first day until now.

TEV: Every time I think of you, I pray for all of you. And when I pray I especially thank my God with joy for the fact that you shared with me in spreading the good news from the first day until now.

The writer in semantics will like to think that one of these translations is better as a translation than the other not just because it reads more like the English that we are familiar with but because it has reached into the deeper structure of the Greek and brought out its underlying meaning. In our ancient biblical texts, however, a special problem arises because very often we cannot know with confidence what the precise meaning of the original passage is. Two or three interpretations of the passage might in fact be possible. In such a situation, the translator working from deep structures might well successfully express one of these possible meanings but in doing so will have excluded or obscured the other possible meaning; in addition the reader will have been deprived of the opportunity of knowing that the passage might not in fact mean what the translator has made it mean. In passages which contain these uncertainties or ambiguities the other method of translation offers an advantage because the translation based on the surface structure of the Greek will reflect in English the ambivalence encountered in the original, and the reader will retain the opportunity of trying to decide what the author meant.

The best way to appreciate the difference between the two methods of translation is to compare them at work in a passage where interpretations have differed. We will use an important passage about the ordering of the church which we will be considering in full in the next chapter. In the first English translation of Acts 6.2 by William Tyndale (1534), the Twelve announce that 'it is not meet that we should leave the word of God and serve at the tables.' Over sixty years later the scholars who produced the *Authorised Version* made what would appear to be a merely pedantic change here by leaving out the definite article and writing 'serve tables'; after all the Greek did not have the article. When the *Authorised Version* in its turn was revised in 1881 the scholars added an alternative translation in the margin which read, 'Or, *minister to tables*'. Thus, while Tyndale's phrase probably sounds better, it almost necessarily makes us think of serving food at the tables whereas the other translations, especially the one in the margin of the Revised Version 1881, suggest to us that the Greek may not have been as clear as that. Now when we turn to twentieth century translations, we find two quite different ideas being put more and more clearly in English. On the one hand we read phrases like 'to wait at table' (*New English Bible*), 'attend to meals' (Moffatt), 'to give out food' (*Jerusalem Bible*) and, on the other hand, phrases like 'to look after the accounts' (Phillips), 'to handle finances' (*Good News*)—the singular nineteenth century translator, Ferrar Fenton, supported this last in writing 'to attend to mere money matters'. A significant difference between all such translations and the Authorised Version is that in designating one particular kind of service the translator is not giving the reader the chance of wondering whether the original author could have been thinking of anything else. In this case the more useful translation would seem to be the one which says plainly what the Greek says, which word for word is 'to serve tables', because this leaves the reader the option of trying to determine whether the writer intended us to understand a service relating to food, a service related to banking, or a service of some other kind altogether. We will be seeing how significant a careful approach to the meaning of this passage can be for understanding what Luke was trying to tell us about this critical moment in his account of a major development in the ordering of the early church. We will next see in regard to a more central question of the ordering of church that our thinking can be substantially affected by how translators lead us to understand what place ministry itself holds within the church's structures.

A fractious comma

In Ephesians 4.12, where a writer in an early Christian church is saying something which is obviously meant to be important about the place of ministry in the church, the translators of the *Revised Standard Version* have had second thoughts between the first edition of their work in 1946 and the second in 1971. (In this verse the *New Revised Standard Version* of 1990 follows the latter.) Between the two editions they dropped a comma. Now a comma is a humble piece of punctuation but it can change the sense of a statement. And that is what happened here. Let us look at the passage first in the version of 1946. The passage is speaking of Christ's gifts to his church. Verse 12 is in italics.

Ephesians 4.11-13
Revised Standard Version (1946):
And his gifts were
that some should be apostles,
some prophets,
some evangelists,
some pastors and teachers,
for the equipment of the saints,
for the work of ministry,
for building up the body of Christ,
until we all attain to the unity of the faith
and of the knowledge of the Son of God....

If one had not been familiar with this passage (and was thus unaware of any controversy about it) and were now asked what the purpose might be of these gifts of apostles and teachers, one would not hesitate to say that the purpose is expressed in the three phrases of verse 12 beginning with 'for'. If then asked to be specific about who does 'the work of ministry' mentioned there, again one would not hesitate to name the people listed as apostles, prophets, evangelists, pastors and teachers. If pushed even further to say what 'the work of ministry' consisted in, one would confidently state that the work of ministry consisted in sustaining and developing the life of faith within the Christian community. Lastly, if this passage were presented as the charter for ministry in the churches of today, one would conclude that ministry is the prerogative of those called pastors or priests, and that it is a role they do not share with anyone else.

Let us look now at how the passage is presented in the second edition of 1971. (The passage is set out for the purpose of emphasising the effect of the punctuation.)

Ephesians 4.11-13
Revised Standard Version (1971):
And his gifts were
that some should be apostles,
some prophets,
some evangelists,
some pastors and teachers,
for the equipment of the saints for the work of ministry,
for building up the body of Christ,
until we all attain to the unity of the faith,
and of the knowledge of the Son of God....

The comma has been taken away after the word 'saints' in the first of three phrases beginning with 'for', and a moment's reflection shows that the program for ministry which one can sketch on the basis of the 1946 translation can no longer be constructed on the basis of the 1971 translation. Let us look at that a little more closely.

In the 1971 translation the gifts to the church are still the various types of teachers, and the ultimate purpose of these gifts of teachers, as the last three lines from this translation continue to show, is the sustaining and developing of the community's faith. But a big difference has appeared in the preceding line where the passage states the immediate purpose of the gift of teachers to the church. The purpose of the teachers is now said to be to equip the saints for the work of ministry. And at a glance we see that the work of ministry thus passes from the teachers to the saints, so that if we take this passage as presented in the translation of 1971 as the charter for ministry in the churches of today ministry is no longer an exclusive prerogative of the pastors and priests but is a work in which all members of the community are to be engaged.

A lot more could be said about the meaning and implications of each of these translations, but a reader new to this section of the letter to the Ephesians or to questions relating to how reliable our translations are will want to know what is going on when from one passage of early Christian Greek two such different views about how the church should be organised and operate can arise.

The short answer to that is that the Greek passage itself has not appeared to translators to be totally clear. (In the Greek manuscripts from which we get our text there is, in fact, no punctuation at all of this kind, and we have to make up our minds about the meaning of the passage solely on the strength of how the words fall.) Translators have been happy enough with the meaning of individual words—although we will see some discrepancy about the odd word 'equipment'—and their problem has been in trying to decide in what way the sentence has been constructed. We have just noticed what a big difference it makes when they choose one kind of sentence structure against another. Some take the three phrases beginning with 'for' as three separate purposes of the pastors, while others join the first and second phrases as one purpose, which switches the role of ministry from pastors to saints.

The first English bibles

Difference of opinion about this point of translation has shown itself for as long as there have been English bibles. Interestingly, the most adventurous version is that in the first printed English New Testament in its final revision by William Tyndale (1535):

> that the sayntes myght have all thinges necessarie to worke and minister with all, to the edifyinge of the body of Christ

Other sixteenth century bibles chose to keep closer to the structure of the Greek phrases until the Authorised Version set a pattern which lasted until the flurry of modern translations. They are worth looking at. (I take the text from *The New Testament Octapla* edited by Luther A. Weigle but show only the date of the original publication.)

Great Bible   to the edifyenge of the saynctes,
(1539)   to the worke and ministracyon,
                    even to the edifyinge of the body of Chryst

Geneva Bible   For the gathering together of the Saintes for the
(1560)   worke of the ministerie, [and] for the edification
                    of the bodie of Christ.

Bishops' Bible (1568)	To the gathering together of the saints, into the worke of the ministration, into the edifying of the body of Christ
Rheims (1582)	to the consummation of the sainctes, unto the worke of the ministerie, unto the edifying of the body of Christ
King James (1611)	for the perfecting of the saints [,]* for the work of the ministry, for the edifying of the body of Christ (*The comma is printed in some editions and omitted in others.)
Revised Version (1881)	for the perfecting of the saints, unto the work of ministering, unto the building up of the body of Christ

Perhaps the main impression one takes from these translations is the variation in respect of the word which the *Revised Standard Version* gave above as 'equipment'. The choices of word at this point fall fairly comfortably into two groups: (1) *perfecting* and *consummation* (which in the Challoner revision of the Rheims version in 1749 became *perfecting*, but both these Roman Catholic versions are from the Latin Vulgate bible), these suggesting that the saints are brought to the peak of their existence or performance as Christians; and (2) *edifying* and *gathering together*, which bring in the idea of preparing the saints for some task. One notices that among modern versions independent of the *Authorised* or *King James Version* the only ones supporting the first idea are Roman Catholic (Spencer, 1940; Confraternity, 1941; Knox, 1946). In this would they be intending to exclude the possibility of the general body of Christians being involved in the work of ministry, thus ensuring that the translation reflects their theological convictions about who are ministers in the church?

The precise meaning in other Roman Catholic translations is difficult to pin down (*Jerusalem, New American, New Jerusalem, Christian Community*), only Lilly (of Kleist and Lilly, 1956) clearly aligning the meaning with that in (2) above, 'thus organising the saints for the work of the ministry which is... ' The most explicit attempt to attribute this meaning to the author of the passage would be in the *New World* translation (1950), 'with a view to the training of the holy ones for ministerial work,' but the idea is clearly contained also in such phrases as the following: 'with a view to fitting his People for the work of the ministry' (*Twentieth Century*, 1901); 'to fit his people for the work of service' (Goodspeed, 1923); 'for the immediate equipment of God's people for the work of service' (Williams, 1937); 'that Christians might be properly equipped for their service' (Phillips, 1958); 'to get his holy people ready to serve as workers' (Beck, 1964); 'to prepare all God's people for the work of Christian service' (*Good News, 1966*); 'to equip the saints for the task of ministering' (*Revised Berkeley*, 1969); 'to prepare God's people for works of service' (*New International Version*, 1973). A refinement appears in the *New English Bible* (1961), retained in its revision (1989), with the idea of 'work in his service'; Heinz W. Cassirer modified even this in *God's New Covenant* (1989), 'to equip God's consecrated ones for the work of serving him.'

The dominant line of interpretation emerging from the modern translations is that the saints do the work of ministry, and this is in close accord with the contemporary view which has occasioned this book that all Christians are ministers because they have been baptized into a ministerial condition. If we move away from translations to sample what people write about the passage, we can find this line of interpretation strongly endorsed. Prominent samples would be from Hans-Ruedi Weber, who is director of bible studies for the World Council of Churches, in *Living in the Image of Christ*, and from Markus Barth, who translated Ephesians and wrote a two volume commentary in the well known Anchor Bible series.

'A Copernican change'

Weber drew attention to the differences at this point of Ephesians in the two editions of the *Revised Standard Version* in much the same way as we have done and made the following comment on the more recent and generally held view (pp. 71-72):

> ... *all* the members of the church have received grace and are therefore called to service or—to say exactly the same

thing—called to ministry (the New Testament uses only one word for 'ministry' and 'service', namely, *diakonia*). This ministry of the church is entrusted to the 'saints', to such ordinary people as are most members of the church.

Weber says that this view, in comparison with the view represented in the earlier translation, 'will mean a Copernican change for many of us.' And just how dramatic a change can be envisaged for the structure and rationale of the churches as a result of implementing this view appears from the title Markus Barth gave to the section of his commentary devoted to the passage. He headed it, 'The Church without Laymen and Priests' (p. 477).

Barth provides a vigorous sketch of this kind of church: 'all saints and the whole church are ... clergymen of God' (p. 481). The church has received one and the same grace for all, which comes in baptism and in effect is 'ordination for participation in the church's ministry.' 'Christ wants, trusts, and equips all members of God's people to be active servants,' so that 'the church consists exclusively of responsible, active, well-equipped saints and servants.' The ' resulting democratic character of the church,' however, 'does not obliterate the roles which specific servants must and may play within the church.' (p. 482) These specific servants are, of course, the various pastors and teachers listed in Ephesians 4.11. They do not form 'a class, rank, or caste' but 'are enlisted and installed for the purpose of "equipping" (all) the saints': the pastor is 'a minister to ministers' (p. 481). Thus there is no one part of the church appointed by God for ministry. To read the passage as if there were a separate ministry —and Barth lists some of the prominent writers who have read it this way, including John Chrysostom, Thomas Aquinas, John Calvin, and the twentieth century scholars Martin Dibelius and Heinrich Schlier—requires what he calls in rather strong language 'arbitrary distortions of the text' (p. 479).

We have now sampled a couple of theologians and a large number of translators putting before us very clearly the idea that all Christians are ministers. And of course they are putting this forward as the view maintained in an early Christian document, the letter to the Ephesians, which is acknowledged by all to distil a lived experience and profound vision of church. Perhaps especially we ought to take note of how widely the view is represented in the modern translations, because it is from the New Testament that teachers, preachers, and leaders and members of discussion groups mainly seek to renew their own vision of church and to identify their roles within it. Small wonder, one might think, that in these last decades the view has become so popular when the opposite view is so thinly represented in commonly used bibles.

It is well for us to keep in mind, therefore, that the idea of a general ministry of all Christians is a thoroughly modern view and that, although it admirably suits the spirit of our democratic age, it is ultimately only as sound as the interpretation of Ephesians 4.11-13 on which it mainly rests. We have already taken note of the fact that in offering his interpretation, Markus Barth acknowledged that Calvin was of a different opinion, and indeed he was, as were all the reformers of his era. Not only their convictions about this but the language in which they expressed them at this point are of interest to us in illustrating how serious the question of ministry was to them and how passionately they protected the prerogatives of the exclusive group who had access to it.

Back to the reformers

Writing in the *Institutes* on Ephesians 4.4-16, Calvin says that what keeps the believers together in one body is 'the ministry of men', whom he calls both the 'guards' to keep the church safe and 'the ministers to whom he has committed this office.' Only through their ministry 'the renewal of the saints is accomplished.' And he utters this strong statement:

> Whoever, therefore, studies to abolish this order and kind of government of which we speak, or disparages it as of minor importance, plots the devastation, or rather the ruin and destruction of the Church. For neither are the light and heat of sun, nor meat and drink, so necessary to sustain and cherish the present life, as is the

apostolical and pastoral office to preserve a Church in the earth.

This is the standard theology of ministry for the reformers. Luther was under no illusions about the necessity of an exclusive ministry, writing in his treatise of 1539 *On the Councils and the Church*, and in reference to this passage from Ephesians, 'The people as a whole cannot do these things, but must entrust or have them entrusted to one person.' The view is encapsulated in the statement about ministry included in the Second Helvetic Confession of the Calvinists in 1566. Here opportunity was taken to compare the notion of the priesthood of all believers, which was the mainspring of so much of the reformed assessment of church, with the notion of ministry. They had no wish that the commonness of one condition, namely priesthood, should provide occasion to erode the exclusiveness of the other prerogative, namely ministry:

> To be sure, Christ's apostles call all who believe in Christ 'priests', but not on account of an office, but because, all the faithful having been made kings and priests, we are able to offer up spiritual sacrifices to God through Christ. [Bible references are here made.] Therefore, the priesthood and the ministry are very different from one another. For the priesthood, as we have just said, is common to all Christians; not so is the ministry.

An historian of the period, James L. Ainslie, writing precisely on *The Doctrines of Ministerial Order in the Reformed Churches of the 16th and 17th Centuries* summarised the convictions of the time in the following paragraph (p. 5):

There is one noteworthy fact at once to be noticed. The Reformers, who were the leaders in the main Reformation movements, when renouncing, and opposing themselves to, the Pope and his hierarchy, and setting aside the Mediaeval Church Orders, did not in the least reject a ministerial order and seek to abolish the Ministry as an institution in the Christian Church. They might have done so. The Reformation was a revolution.

Much was being cast down. The Order of the Ministry might have been thus treated, and might have been rejected in every form. There were tendencies of that kind at work in the commotion of the times to decry and denounce any Order of Ministry in the Church. But the great Reformation leaders not only saw the usefulness of having an order of ministry for the Churches of the reformation which were being constituted, but they believed in its immense importance and divine sanction.

'Precious pearls'

One minister and scholar of the period whose mind in these matters, in particular as they relate to our passage in Ephesians, we can get in close touch with is Paul Bayne, 'sometime preacher of God's word at St Andrew's in Cambridge', who died in 1617 and whose 'entire commentary' on Ephesians was published in the following year and republished in London as late as 1866. In regard to the three phrases in verse 12 of chapter 4, firstly, Bayne does not hesitate to see three distinct ends or purposes for the pastors and teachers of verse 11; he expresses this effectively:

> The ends follow, which are set down three ways, in regard of three kinds of persons to whom the function of the ministry hath reference.
> 1. In regard of the people: it is to repair them.
> 2. In regard of themselves that are pastors and teachers: it is that they should labour, and not make holiday.
> 3. In regard of Christ: that his body may be built.

If we already see from here that the ministry is not something pertaining to the people, we ought to pause briefly, secondly, to see how forcefully Bayne asserts that this is part of the doctrine about church and ministry in this passage. He writes:

> In the next place, he saith he gave (not all) to be apostles, but some. Whence observe, that the calling of ministry is not common to all, but to some only that are good in the eyes of Christ for such purpose. ... For look, as all the body

is not an eye, so all the body of Christ is not a minister, whose office it is to be in this mystical body, as the eye is in the natural.

In the clear eyes of Paul Bayne, Puritan, ministers of the gospel are 'the special favours of Christ' and 'the precious pearls that Christ doth send.'

'A large-scale paradigm shift'

We could take this sort of enquiry through the succeeding centuries of scholarship and up to the present, mentioning Heinrich Schlier and Helmut Merklein in particular who have written close studies of these passages. Our purpose at the moment, however, is not so much to resolve a dispute about who has a ministerial role according to the author of the letter to the Ephesians, as to illustrate what Hans-Ruedi Weber has called 'the Copernican change' producing the predominant modern view that all are ministers.

The appeal of this new churchwide ministry is especially strong to many of today's Christians who are deeply committed to the works of the gospel but whose churches maintain a rigid demarcation between ordained ministers and the rest of the baptized. These are churches commonly said to be hierarchical in structure, like the Roman Catholic Church, the Church of England, and the Orthodox churches. In the Roman Catholic Church, which historically has clearly exhibited both the exclusiveness of ministerial authority and its strong lines of power, non-ordained members have become in recent years increasingly involved in administrative roles which had previously been filled by clergy and, beyond this, in roles of a churchly or ministerial kind which had previously been thought of as the domain of the ordained. One influence in this opening of these opportunities to the non-ordained is certainly the current shrinkage in the supply of ordained ministers, but a more significant one is the sheer enthusiasm of the non-ordained for these tasks. And to enthusiasm, born of new visions of church after the Second Vatican Council, they have added a wide range of professional training and qualifications, in some areas many being more suitably equipped than their ordained employers and colleagues.

For such people, the experience of working within the limited possibilities provided by the hierarchical confines of their church is itself an impetus to broaden and deepen their appreciation of a rationale which will make their work for church more effective and more churchly. The rationale of a churchwide ministry clearly offers them this opportunity. In those regional sectors of the Roman Catholic Church where the level of education is advanced, aspirants to churchly work can project this rationale not only with seeming theological propriety but to increasing political effect. Their numbers and responsibilities are such that their heightened perceptions of the potential scope of responsibilities open to the non-ordained in the church do indeed filter into the broader community. Their principal impact, however, is probably upon the thinking within the hierarchical levels themselves where bishops, especially those with directly pastoral briefs or sentiment, feel the need to accommodate the new professionals and to build the new perceptions into the way they run their churches. Even to voice puzzlement as to how in the future, with this expansion of churchly activity beyond the parameters of hierarchy, we are going to be able to talk about ministry in a traditional ecclesiastical sense is itself merely to provide further evidence of what has already happened to that kind of talk. While Pope John Paul II himself, in his response to the Roman Synod on the Laity in 1987, revealed that an enquiry continues into this question, an observer would probably conclude that the broad use of ministry, inclusive of all members of the church, has won the day.

Shortly we will examine one instance of how effectively this inclusive sense of ministry can be put to work within a theology of church rooted in hierarchical structures. Before doing so we can usefully observe the changing theological climate which favours the growth of this inclusive sense within the Roman Catholic community. There, within, as we saw, the ferment of ministers and ministries, one of the most respected and influential studies of ministry has been Thomas O'Meara's *Theology of*

Ministry which includes the following much cited definition of ministry (p. 142):

> Christian ministry is the public activity of a baptized follower of Jesus Christ flowing from the Spirit's charism and an individual personality on behalf of a Christian community to witness to, serve and realise the kingdom of God.

Of the several elements within this definition which might be considered novel in the light of the traditional notion of ministry I draw attention to its essentially charismatic nature—and that without further comment here—and, of importance to our present purpose, to the attribution of ministry to every baptized person. A ministerial empowerment through baptism is fundamental to the theology developed by O'Meara: 'A theology of ministry on behalf of the community begins with baptism.' Since all are baptized, the church is 'a community which is essentially ministerial' (p. 141); baptism is 'an initiation into a new eschatological life which intrinsically includes ministry' (p. 139). Expanding from this base in *The Lay-Centered* Church Leonard Doohan sees hope of structural change filtering upwards from grass-roots groups which will gradually bring an end to the hierarchical monopoly over governing and teaching (pp. 130-131), an end too of 'inappropriate hierarchical control over ministry' (p. 133) in a church where each member has 'a permanent commitment to ministry that results from baptism' (p. 45). James and Evelyn Whitehead call this new movement an 'imaginative broadening' of a ministry which must no longer be seen as 'an elite calling reserved to those with a special vocation' (*The Emerging Laity*, p. 159); the years ahead must see further efforts, beyond those already undertaken at and since the Second Vatican Council, 'to purify past authorisations of ministry and leadership' (p. 149). Within the same dynamic but more forcefully William Rademacher speaks of these past ministries as not only past but 'clearly obsolete' and 'a useless burden' and 'dead weight' on the backs of 'the baptized ministers', who are called 'to minister in a truly pastoral way to the needs of today' (*Lay Ministry*, p 228).

These are widely disseminated views in the English-speaking churches of the Roman communion which have been long developing within the United States. I would like to complement them by reference to an address entitled 'Lay Ministry: Living Its Questions' by H. Richard McCord, who spoke as associate director of the National Conference of Catholic Bishops' Secretariat for Laity and Family Life in the United States and thus represents the voice of the non-ordained Christian professionally engaged in questions of ministry (*Origins*, 19 April 1990). As the title of his address indicates, the author is aware of the as yet unresolved questions affecting 'lay ministry' in a hierarchical church, and, as the official policy seems now to be, he proposes going along with this incertitude on the grounds that by living and working within a ministerial framework we have a better chance of seeing workable answers emerge than if we sat down to write out in advance a set of definitions. By pursuing this line one would anticipate the working model of 'lay ministry' becoming in time the only workable one, and in such a case the opportunity to develop a strategy based on definition of roles will have passed. The problem of how to talk of a ministry common to both ordained and non-ordained often attracts the attention of writers, and was the centre of considerable comment at the Roman synod on the laity in 1987, Cardinal Hume of Westminster in particular attempting to clarify usage. Thomas O'Meara, in his study just referred to, has expressed his impatience with the 'confused, sterile, even duplicitous' character of ministry's language (p. 144), while Richard McBrien attempted in his *Ministry* to establish a consistent terminology (pp. 11-12).

In his address McCord is conscious that he is describing 'a large-scale paradigm shift in the way we have come to understand church', and that the 'fresh questions and new problems' relate to a 'shift in language' which has occurred in the years since the Second Vatican Council. That these questions and problems remain as yet unresolved is clear from the widespread dissatisfaction with the nature of the agenda and of the debate at the Roman synod on laity and from the fact that Pope John Paul II chose the occasion to establish a commission whose brief was to examine the differentiation of ministry within the ordained and non-ordained sectors of the church. His own postsynodal letter *Christifideles laici* of 1989 acknowledged the problem which the commission was to face but sought to relieve the increasing pressure which the concept of lay ministry was putting on official ministry by teaching that, whereas lay ministry is grounded in baptism and confirmation, ordained ministry, which is essentially different, is grounded in the sacrament of order.

McCord moved cautiously through such official teachings, pointing out in particular that no longer was lay involvement in ministry by way of delegation from the hierarchy, as was the language and thinking earlier in this century when the concept of lay apostolate was in vogue, but was rather 'grounded ... in the same source as the hierarchy's, namely, in the one ministry of Christ'; once this participation itself came to be spoken of as ministry, the shift 'included the possibility of laity being called ministers.'

The main thing which the language of ministry does is to emphasize that all the people of God hold in common a respon-sibility for the mission of the church. ... Ministry belongs to the whole church.

The ministry

A prominent champion of this theology of ministry in the inau-gural stages of the ecumenical movement was John A. Mackay, a Scotsman of the Free Presbyterian Church who had been a missionary in South America and became an energetic President of Princeton Theological Seminary, New Jersey. In 1938 he had been invited to prepare a series of lectures to be presented in the University of Edinburgh. War postponing the presentation, it was not until January 1948 that the opportunity returned. That month heralded the year in which the World Council of Churches was to be inaugurated at the assembly in Amsterdam. Mackay was himself a member of the Provisional Committee of the World Council, he was chairman of the mother body, the International Missionary Council, and for years was to be on the Central Committee of the new World Council. At the beginning of 1948, Mackay assessed that the occasion of his lectures called for a study on the nature of church.

With great deliberation he called the lectures *God's Order,* because his purpose was to expound the vision of church 'embraced in, and guaranteed by, the eternal Purpose of God' as put forward by Paul in the letter to the Ephesians, a piece of the Christian scriptures which had been central to his life since boyhood. He published the revised lectures as a book under that title in 1953 with the subtitle, *The Ephesian Letter and This Present Time.* (My copy is the fifth printing of 1964, evidence of the impact the book was making.) I draw attention to the portentous character Mackay attributed to a right understanding of this letter because in his treatment of the statement which has engaged us in this chapter, Ephesians 4.11-13, he called strongly for the recognition in the churches of the broad vision of ministry which we have been describing. That vision has long since become the vision of ministry within the World Council of Churches, is enshrined, as we saw in our opening pages, in its statement *Baptism, Eucharist and Ministry,* and is causing a ferment of attempts to come to grips with it in the Roman Catholic Church.

Mackay opened his treatment of the passage with the unequivocal statement that the task of pastors in the church is to equip the saints 'in order that they too, in a non-professional but effective sense, may become 'ministers'', proceeding at once to state: 'No passage in the Bible is more crucial than this for the welfare and mission of the Christian Church today.' He is aware of the contrary interpretation, namely, that the ministry belongs to the pastors instead of to the saints, but, encouraged by the trend in the modern translations which we have illustrated, confidently asserts that the meaning he perceives appears clearly as an expression of 'the general tenor of Paul's thought'. The idea that the saints 'may engage in ministering, that they too may be servants' is 'startling, but decisive': 'Every Christian is called to be a minister, a servant, a priest' (pp.149-151). The perception here was the fountainhead of Mackay's vision of church. For this reason, no doubt, he chose this section of his book for advance publication in the journal which he had founded at Princeton, *Theology Today* (January 1953).

We notice that at this crucial point the 'ministry' which the writer of Ephesians makes basic to church becomes one with the 'service' of every Christian. Shortly after the publication of Mackay's book its theme was independently developed in another influential study *A Theology of the Laity* by Hendrik Kraemer, late director of the Ecumenical Institute in Bossey, Switzerland, whose work in the cause of laity is well known. Kraemer's study was pioneering in a number of ways, nowhere more than in the 'prophetic one-sidedness' of its call to break the inertia which bound the churches to a view of ministry as exclusively institutional (pp. 166-169). Like Mackay, Kraemer roots his conviction about ministry in Ephesians 4.11-12, a correct understanding of which, as he wrote (p. 140),

> rules out the use of the text as a corroboration for the condition of the Church as we know it by tradition, viz. the 'ministry', the diakonia as a specialized sphere. Of this specialised sphere the Church in its primitive, fluid state was scarcely conscious. All the stress was the diakonia, the ministry of the whole membership, because the Church as a whole stood under the same token as its Lord, i.e. 'servantship'.

As a consequence (p. 143),

> The ministry of the ordained clergy and the ministry of the laity are both aspects of the same diakonia, each in their proper sphere and calling.

Kraemer would have been pleased indeed to see just such a scheme of ministry embodied in *A Plan of Union* commended by the Consultation on Church Union (USA) in 1970 (Chapter VII, 'To Be Ministers of Christ'):

> The ministry of the church is one. The ministries of the ordained and the unordained are aspects of this one ministry. Lay persons and the ordained share the same basic vocation to become free and responsible members of the new human community.

What Kraemer's concentration on a universal ministry does for us is to remind us that in all modern discussion of ministry we are not using the English word *ministry* in any recognisably historical English sense but are importing into it a sense and a set of values which linguists and theologians have attributed this century to a Greek word used by the first Christians, namely, *diakonia*. This is the word that occurs at Ephesians 4.12, 'for the work of ministry/*diakonia*', and Kraemer calls it 'that profound, revolutionary word' (p. 187). The word is indeed revolutionary if by its import we are justified in speaking univocally of the ministries of the ordained and the non-ordained. This book, like its academic predecessor, *Diakonia: Re-interpreting the Ancient Sources*, argues, however, that from a purely linguistic point of view we are not justified in making this revolutionary shift in the way we think about ministry, and in the following chapters we will review the arguments in looking at how first Luke, then Paul and other early Christian writers spoke of and understood ministry/*diakonia*. We can conclude this chapter, which has reported on much that the revolution has already achieved in contemporary thinking about church and ministry, by returning briefly to a central conviction of the reformers at the time of the other great revolution in church and ministry.

When Calvin sketched the theme of the letter to the Ephesians in the introduction to his commentary on that letter, he stated that the fourth chapter was about 'the ministry by which God reigns among us', and this a ministry of preaching, of which he observes at 4.10:

> The sum of it is that because the Gospel is preached by certain men appointed to that office, this is the economy by which the Lord wishes to govern His Church, that it may remain safe in this world, and ultimately obtain its complete perfection.

3: Ministry in Luke's Church

In this chapter we will begin looking at the various activities which early Christian writers called 'ministry' or *diakonia*. Luke will be first, not because he was the first to write this way—far from it—but because in his Acts of the Apostles we are in touch with a sense of church approximating ours, or so we tend to think of it. He is also a writer who has revealed himself both in this part of his composition and in its prelude, his Gospel, to be sensitive to the values which Greek writers in all ages had chosen *diakonia* and its kindred words to give expression to. We will see him writing of the ministry of the Eleven in Acts 1, associated with which is the ministry of Paul (Acts 20.24; 21.19), then of the ministry of the Seven in Acts 6, and of the form of ministry which is delegation between churches in Acts 11.29 and 12.25.

The overarching ministry

The 'work of ministry' which we have been looking at in Ephesians 4.12 is by no means the only place where there is talk of ministry. When Luke sets out in the first chapter of Acts to recount the wondrous story of how the word of God spread around the world from Jerusalem to the ends of the earth (Acts 1.8), Peter names the whole undertaking 'this ministry' (1.17); then, to make the number of apostles twelve again, the gathering examines the credentials of two candidates for the vacancy in the 'office' (1.20: *episkopen*), and pray that the Lord will show in the casting of lots which one he has elected to take a place in 'this *ministry/diakonia* and apostleship' (1.25). Many chapters in the story later, when Paul summons the elders of the church of Ephesus to meet him at Miletus, and there makes his farewell to them at what was to prove the end of his missionary journeys as recorded by Luke, Paul anticipates grave dangers to his person

35

on his return to Jerusalem but declares his determination to complete 'the *ministry/diakonia* which I received from the Lord Jesus' (Acts 20.24). And when, at the end of the long journey, he presents himself in Jerusalem to James and all the elders he makes a full report of what 'God had done among the Gentiles through his *ministry/diakonia*' (Acts 21.19). Thus both at the beginning of the undertaking, that is, when the Lord commissioned the Eleven, and then at its consummation, when Paul reported to Jerusalem on his achievement, the writer Luke chooses to have us think of it as a ministry.

For Luke, accordingly, ministry is that office or charge which was laid upon the apostles, who were the first and remained for him the foundational proclaimers of the word, and in the carrying out of which under the Lord's mandate the church was established, secured and propagated. The process of inducting Matthias into this ministry was carried out under the leadership of one already commissioned in ministry, and included verifying the candidate's credentials as a witness to Jesus and his resurrection, his recommendation by the whole church of 120 persons, public prayer, and the casting of lots. The selection of the candidate through the casting of lots signifies that the selection was the prerogative of God and was special to the need of the church at this moment, namely, to fill the vacancy among the apostles. At the same time the account reveals Luke's conviction that the church has a prime responsibility to maintain the authenticity of its ministry. In the case of Paul the community has no direct part in the process because he was the Lord's own 'chosen instrument' (9.15) brought into the community from outside; this circumstance gives even greater emphasis to the sacred character of ministry, to the weight of its authority, to the demands it lays on those who are charged with it, and to its effectiveness in mediating God's saving purposes.

The management of ministry

At one moment in the early course of the ministry established by the Lord, the Twelve discern the need to increase the number of those engaged in ministry. Luke has already presented a picture of the new believers at Pentecost, about three thousand souls now, attending to 'the teaching of the apostles', to fellowship, to the breaking of bread, and to prayer (2.42). He immediately enlarges on this picture and has them continuing in a sense of being together in their faith and life, day by day going together to the Temple, and then breaking bread in their homes, generously and happily sharing together, and praising God (2.44-47). Further on again, as the believers continue to increase in numbers and build their fellowship, we read of the power of the apostles' testimony to the resurrection of the Lord (4.32-35). Finally, after the violent intrusion upon this scene of the apostles' imprisonment and flogging, they once more are 'teaching and preaching' in the temple and in their homes 'every day' (5.42).

In this picture Luke emphasizes constant attention to their ministry by the Twelve. We notice that the Twelve are teaching both in the temple and in houses. We bear this in mind when we read Luke's next statement at 6.1, which tells us that with the still increasing numbers of believers, among whom are people who spoke Greek instead of the native Aramaic, Greek widows are being overlooked. Widows were always a special group in Jewish and early Christian communities—on their increasingly significant place among Christians see Bonnie Bowman Thurston's *The Widows: A Women's Ministry in the Early Church*—and they attracted particular care because their widowhood isolated them socially and rendered them economically insecure. As well, they were largely illiterate. In addition these Greek-speaking widows were unable to understand the Aramaic language the new teachers used. Indeed, with the apostles so busy among the Jews, and with numbers of them not being speakers of Greek, the widows could hardly have avoided being overlooked in what Luke here calls 'the daily ministry' (6.1. In *Hellenists and Hebrews*, p. 26, Craig C. Hill gives scant attention to his own query about this point of language). As a result they were not receiving from the apostles the teaching every believer had a right to. This was bad enough but, given their special claims as widows within the new fellowship, the neglect was intolerable.

That is Luke's picture. Once they received the complaint, the Twelve proposed a solution to the gathering of the disciples. 'It is not right,' they began,' that we should give up the word of God to minister at tables.' (6.2) Readers of the English at this point are inclined to think that the Twelve are referring to waiting on the widows at a meal; certainly our translations encourage us to think like that because, as we noted in the preceding chapter, they usually present us with a phrase like 'serving at tables', which comes on top of the phrase frequently translated at 6.1 as 'the daily distribution' instead of 'the daily ministry'. But Luke's picture does not allow us to shift our focus from the real work of ministry to works of social service. After the scenes of continuous and growing fellowship which Luke has been putting before the reader—and the one violation of the fellowship was such a contradiction to it that its perpetrators fell dead (5.1-10)—the reader must not be allowed to envisage that a group with such claims on fellowship as widows, whether Jewish or Greek, would have been overlooked in the matter of food or other necessities. Rather, Luke is still writing about the ministry which he has had constantly to the fore. The problem which 'the daily ministry' of 6.1 presents to his Twelve is that it is carried on mainly in the temple, where the crowds of disciples had room to meet with them and the crowds of interested, potential Jewish believers could hear their expositions, but where the Greek widows would not venture or even understand if they did. Nor were the widows free to visit the apostles in their homes; and even there the preponderance of Jewish disciples would require teaching in the native language.

After consideration of this serious problem, one thing the Twelve were sure of. They could not commit themselves to taking their ministry to the widows in their houses, teaching them there while, like other groups in the fellowship, they were gathered together to share food and praise God around their tables. 'It is not right,' they said, 'that we should leave aside the public proclamation of the word to carry out our ministry during mealtimes of the widows.' Readers who like to consult a Greek Testament will notice that in the phrase here Luke has omitted the preposition for ministering *at* tables; the reader may even be using a translation which registers this by translating 'to serve tables' (*Revised Standard Version*) instead of 'serve at the tables'

(Tyndale). Luke's omission of the preposition is no accident, for in the omission he is displaying precisely the difference between serving at tables, in the expression of which the Greek language uses the preposition, and carrying out one's ministry in the vicinity of tables, to express which the Greek language does not require a preposition; he intends us to understand that the Twelve will not be ministering their teaching to these small groups of women on the occasion of their gatherings around their tables. (To *minister [at] tables* in Greek thus has a different meaning from to *serve [at] tables* in English.) The priority in the Twelve's 'ministry and apostleship', according to Luke, must remain the lengthy addresses to the crowds in the spacious surrounds of the temple, expounding the meaning of the scriptures, which were 'the word of God'. (In passing we need to note that some writers on this passage like to think of the tables as places where the financial business of supporting the fellowship took place; when Luke wanted to give us a picture of these dealings, however, he suggested a market scene with the apostles squatting while donors laid contributions 'at their feet' [5.35] from which others then received what they needed.)

The rest of what the Twelve had to announce to the assembly flows from understanding their opening statement in this way. The brethren were to select men 'of good repute, full of the Spirit and of wisdom' (6.3), in other words, men cut out to be preachers. The Twelve reserved to themselves the right of appointing these to the new task required within the fellowship. The assembly were only too happy to put forward seven Greek men; these were presented to the apostles, who laid hands on them in prayer as the sign of their appointment. The apostles were freed to return to long prayers of praise in the temple and to 'the ministry of the word' which had been bringing such fruits for the Lord there. They had closed the loophole which had developed without their noticing in the increasingly diverse membership of the fellowship, and they had done a momentous thing. They had brought within their own mandate to preach the gospel, a mandate or *diakonia* which had been given to them by the Lord himself, a group of men who had not accompanied them during all the time that the Lord Jesus went in and out among them (see 1.21).

Thus, in Luke's vision of church, 'the word of God increased' (6.7) because the church took upon itself the task of controlling the supply and quality of its ministers. Stephen, one of the new Seven, was to reappear in the story immediately, 'full of grace and power' (6.8), far from the quiet homes of the Greek widows but demonstrating the capacity of the newly instituted preacher to be faithful unto death in proclaiming the word of the Lord. The next preacher to be included by Luke in this chronicle of the spreading word is another of the Seven, Philip, who took 'the good news of Jesus' (8.36) further afield, beginning in the hills of Samaria and then along the coasts of Palestine from Gaza to Caesarea, where he was remembered as 'the evangelist' (21.8). And the next is the Lord's own selection and appointment, Saul of Tarsus, who is to be the Lord's 'vessel to carry [his] name' (9.15) to peoples, rulers, and communities of Jews in lands beyond.

From Acts 6 we thus learn that for Luke ministry is the work both of proclaiming the word to unbelievers and of nurturing the word among believers; it is a responsibility of certain individuals who have been selected for their suitability by the community but have been inducted into their responsibilities with prayer and ritual by the incumbents of ministry. Luke probably suggests that the inculturation of ministry is the condition of its effectiveness; he clearly proposes that purveying the word of God is the inalienable duty of a church, that it is the essence of its ministry, and that ministry's mandate necessarily extends to keeping ministry versatile; finally he establishes that the tradition of ministry is the assurance of its integrity and of its fidelity to its divine mandate.

A confirming ministry

One other form of ministry is reported by Luke, and we will later see how this form of ministry is important also in the estimation of Paul. On this occasion Luke involves Paul in fact, and with him Barnabas. The word has now spread through Phoenicia to Antioch, then over the sea to Cyprus and Cyrene. As the church in Jerusalem heard of this progress, they sent Barnabas to Antioch in a spirit of fellowship. Delighted with the growth he saw,

Barnabas sought out Paul in Tarsus and recruited him as a co-worker in Antioch in teaching the ever-increasing numbers.

The next development brought out in these disciples, who were Greek-speaking and were the first group to be known by the name of 'Christians' (11.26), a strong sense of their bonding with the Jewish church in Jerusalem from which the word had originated. A prophet had announced that famine was imminent, and the church in Antioch was sensitive at once to the likely needs of its sister church in the south. Each one of the disciples went on putting aside whatever could be spared—Luke's phrasing here (11.29) is awkward to reproduce in English but is emphasising that each disciple did something in this cause—and then they all 'determined [a word for a determination taken in council] to send *representatives* on a delegation to their brothers living in Judea. And this they did [in due course, as the hardship began to bite and their means had been put together], consigning *the contribution* to the Elders by the hand of Barnabas and Saul.'

From the way Luke has put this, let us see what the event has meant for him. A couple of explanatory notes have already been added to the translation, and the first of these, which is to do with 'determined', sets the tone for what follows. We can be sure of this from the solemn occasions for which Luke uses this word elsewhere (Acts 2.23; 10.42; 17.31; Luke 22.22). Decisions about providing assistance to the fellowship in Jerusalem, a region which was always likely to suffer more than most in times of shortages, had been taken instinctively by each of the Christians in Antioch; after a year of ministry from Barnabas, the teacher whom the church in Jerusalem had provided for them, they were keenly aware of the character and good heart of the older church and conscious too of what that church and their own had received in common. Their desire was not only to see that their donation got to Jerusalem, but that from the manner in which it was delivered the church in Jerusalem would draw the added consolation and encouragement of knowing that a thriving and spirited fellowship had developed in the great city of Antioch from initiatives which the Jerusalem church had taken. The church in Jerusalem would be assured that non-Jews made good fellows in the Spirit.

Hence Luke draws upon the language of deputation; at the level of a deputation the young church would be showing to the senior church its maturity, its sense of fellowship in the Spirit, its appreciation of what it had received in the grace of the gospel, and its respect. To 'send' is the first of these words; it has no grammatical object, and in this connection commonly had none in Greek. Our translations, unfortunately, have not represented the idea behind this; since the first, they have almost always added an object, as in 'to send succour', from the earlier times, and from the time of King James 'to send relief'. This idea they have apparently taken from the neighbouring phrase, which is 'into ministry/*diakonia*'. Here a note in the margin of the annotated Geneva Bible (1602) perhaps provides a clue to how the idea of relief got into the passage: because the Greek word *diakonia* also became the word for *diaconate*, it suggested the supposed work by deacons of providing succour or relief, so that the marginal note comments on 'succour', 'That is, that thereof the Deacons might succour the poore...' The curious thing is that just one chapter later, when Barnabas and Paul are said to have finished their 'ministry/*diakonia*' (12.25), the same translators turned at first to 'office' (Tyndale and the next three bibles) and thereafter to 'ministry' (*King James*), 'ministration' (*Revised Version*), and latterly 'mission' (*Revised Standard Version*). Clearly there is a strange inconsistency in these two translations of the same word in the same context at 11.29 and 12.25, and any reader will wonder at the versatility of a word which says 'relief' and 'mission' at the turn of a page. The fact is, of course, that Luke is writing of 'mission' in both places, the disciples determining 'to send on a mission'; hence the word 'representatives' supplied in the translation above.

Next we note the level at which the delegation is to operate, it being directed to 'the Elders'. The reverence in which the Christians of Antioch hold these figures requires that their own representation be at the highest level, which is why the two foremost teachers in the community of Antioch, Barnabas and Paul, are put forward as the delegates. The first and more senior of these is the man known to the authorities of the Jerusalem church because he was their trusted emissary to Antioch, while the second, once feared by them (9.26), represents the new Christian who makes up the new church, himself a Jew but a man of two worlds.

These two short notes by Luke about the reaction of the church in Antioch to impending hardship in the church in Jerusalem (11.29-30 and 12.25) are more than gestures to the history of his times. They are his statement about how one church should see itself in relation to another. Differences in geography—and these were great—and differences in race and culture—which were greater—counted for nothing when the common bond was the Spirit which graced both. When one wished to communicate with the other, even if the occasion was to assist the other, the style of the communication would announce to both communities the perceptions they shared of their new dignity before the Lord. On this ground this delegation has been presented by Luke as a ministry or *diakonia* in the church. The ministry is established as the result of a consultative process, and achieves the high status of ministry—in this case of ministerial delegation—because the authority of the church endorses it. It is a ministry which confirms the church and which publicises the widespread gifts of its Lord. We shall shortly see how Paul also encouraged and took part in such ministry in other churches, and in chapter 6 we shall see why both he and Luke chose to use the word *diakonia* as its name.

4: The Minister Paul

Paul's writings reveal even more than Luke's a predilection for naming the process by which the gospel is established as a ministry. He also goes a step further than Luke and introduces the word *minister* (*diakonos*) to designate the one responsible for making the process work. This seems to be a simple enough step to have taken—and it will bring us into the rich field where we will be able to see various Christian ministers at work—but it does make us wonder why Luke himself, writing at a later time, did not himself ever write of the Christian minister. Perhaps there is a message there, too, which we can try to decipher later.

The essential ministry

Paul sees the whole disclosure by God that the Law has been replaced by the Spirit as a 'ministry' (2 Corinthians 3.7-9, *diakonia* in this passage often being translated as 'dispensation' or 'ministration', both of which are helpful). His own role in bringing an acceptance of this to people is his 'ministry of reconciliation', whereby the people are reconciled through Christ to God (2 Corinthians 5.18). He received this 'ministry' by the mercy of God, and is therefore confident about accomplishing it (2 Corinthians 4.1). Nonetheless he works hard to ensure that no obstacle will fall in the way of 'the ministry' or dispensation (2 Corinthians 6.3). He holds his 'ministry' up for admiration (Romans 11.13).

Obviously ministry is the central reality of Paul's involvement in Christ, and his word *diakonia* itself embraces much. It speaks of a process which God has been involved in during all his past dealings with the chosen people; in comparison with the present dispensation of the Spirit and of righteousness, the earlier dispensation had been one of death and condemnation (2 Corinthians 3.7-9). Ministry is a process which requires human collaboration, in the first instance that of Moses, and in the present new bounty of God Paul has a role within it. To have received this ministry is to have received a gracious endowment from God. To have received this ministry is at the same time a pressing responsibility because it constitutes God's access to other men and women and provides men and women with their access to God. If Christ's achievement is to be realized in the experience of individual human beings, its reconciling power must be made available to them in ministry. Ministry is truly admirable; it is awe-inspiring.

Paul the minister

In a very personal sense Paul locks himself into this process he has called ministry by assuming—and, as occasion arises, vigorously defending—the title of minister. This we see first in 1 Corinthians 3.5, where both he and Apollos are so named. Today's readers will normally find this title translated 'servants', which is hardly eyecatching and would not seem to rate the claim to be a title of office within the grand scale of ministry. To Greek ears, however, the title minister/*diakonos* rang with authority and exactly suited the role Paul cast himself in. When we read back into chapter two of this first letter to the Corinthians we are presented with the high estimation Paul has of himself purveying his message 'in demonstration of the Spirit and power' (verse 4), proclaiming 'the testimony' or 'the mystery' of God (verse 1), 'a secret and hidden wisdom of God, which God decreed before the ages for our glorification' (verse 7), 'what no eye has seen , nor ear heard...' (verse 9), 'interpreting spiritual truths to those who possess the Spirit' (verse 13). To establish a claim to a role in this program of truly cosmic proportions and to settle the disabling squabbling among the Corinthians about the relative merits of the teachers who had been putting the program to them, Paul believed he had only to make clear that the supposed rivals were in fact entitled to be both recognized and received as 'ministers' (1 Corinthians 3.5). Such was the import and power of the word. It said at once to the mind of the ordinary Corinthian that the one to whom it belonged as a title was in a privileged role and came among them endowed with another world's authority.

The importance of this word to him in his vocabulary of the office of the Christian preacher and pastor is even more forcefully brought home to us by the way he uses the title in a bitter and more serious dispute at a slightly later stage in the early history of the Christian community in Corinth. Large pieces of his correspondence composed to finalise the dispute are put together in what we know as the second letter to the Corinthians. In one section he confronts the Corinthian Christians themselves because they have been turning aside from his teaching and becoming attracted to a different kind of preaching to which they had been exposed in Paul's absence by an unidentified group of missionaries unfriendly to Paul and critical of his methods. Paul believes he can re-establish his credibility and authority if he can get the Corinthians to see that he has in fact been a minister to them. Behind this stratagem is his realisation that by acknowledging this one title they will have eliminated the possibility that his rivals could also be authentic Christian preachers.

These passages, from 2 Corinthians 2.14 to 6.13, would take us more space and time to examine closely than we really need to use. (For a close study of these and related passages see my chapter 10, 'Spokesmen and Emissaries of Heaven' in *Diakonia: Re-interpreting the Ancient Sources.*) All we need to remind ourselves of here is that in this critical encounter with one of the earliest groups of Christian believers the *apostle* of whom we know most swung his argument around his claim to be the *minister.* His opening claim says enough to this effect to satisfy doubts any reader may have about how significant this title is for him here. He writes that it is 'God who has qualified us to be ministers of a new covenant' (2 Corinthians 3.6). And throughout he keeps coming back to these *minister/ministry* words, lacing them intricately into a complex but coherent and powerful argument. (See the occurrences of the words at 2 Corinthians 3.3,5,6,7,8,9; 4.1; 5.18; 6.3,4.)

In a later piece of the correspondence, again now included in our 2 Corinthians at chapters 10-13, Paul continues the debate, this time turning a lot of his efforts towards discrediting the intruders into the Corinthian church. And in what aspect in particular of their activity as preachers among the Corinthians does he seek most to discredit them? In their claim that they are 'ministers of Christ' (2 Corinthians 11.23). We thus see that establishing oneself as a minister was a condition of taking up a preaching role within the community. On this occasion Paul sought to discredit his opponents' claim with more sustained vigor and passion than perhaps he ever used elsewhere. In his effort, as well as effectively championing his own career as 'minister' (11.23-28), he did not hesitate to name his critics and rivals 'ministers' of Satan (11.15).

Paul's opponents established their claims on their performance—and they were good presenters—and on letters of accreditation, which they could produce. Paul could not better them on either ground. He conceded their skills, and could only contest the question of accreditation from a seemingly weak position. He had no letters of accreditation; his status was unique because his role as minister had come to him in the call of the Lord himself. While this awareness of the Lord's call gave conviction to Paul in his ministry, it is not the stuff claims can be made out of. This is what led Paul to invite the Corinthians to go back into what they had experienced under his guidance and teaching, because there, he told them, they would discover, in their own awareness of the Spirit and in the surety of enlightenment, that they had indeed been in touch with the God whom Jesus the Lord had made available. In this discovery they will have found also 'the man whom the Lord commends' (2 Corinthians 10.18).

A minister's code

The kind of accreditation Paul possessed is the most credible of all. But it is not immune to challenge. Opponents can circumvent it, as in Paul's case, by producing alternative forms in accord with society's norms in such matters. Challenges on these lines can undermine people's confidence in their own experience. At the other extreme, as the stories of false religious and political messiahs illustrate, charlatans and deluded visionaries can so exploit the credulous that these people lose confidence also in what had once seemed sure leadership. Paul was aware of the threats from both these sides and, in regard at least to his collaborators, insisted, as we shall see, that their accreditation as ministers be known. The very word *minister/diakonos* implied to the Greek person that the minister has the authority of the one who has commissioned him or her. This is what requires that the accreditation and the authority of the minister be recognized as the first characteristics that ministry in a church should display.

Because Paul lacked the normal external credentials and had not entirely succeeded in re-establishing his credibility among the Corinthians with his appeal to their experience of the gospel (2 Corinthians 3-6), his last recorded stratagem was to hold up for public scrutiny his career as a 'minister/*diakonos*' (2 Corinthians 11.23-28). In doing this he was not merely flaunting his courage, his sufferings, and the dangers he had exposed himself to in the course of his ministry, but was pressing an argument on the ground of what Greeks knew a minister should do. This was that a minister must get his message through. To be acclaimed 'faithful' to one's charge, as Paul later acclaimed Tychichus and Epaphras (Colossians 1.7; 4.7; and see Ephesians 6.21; 1 Timothy 1.12), was the highest commendation a 'minister' could receive. Paul could show from events in his career which were matters of public knowledge that he had taken himself to the point of exhaustion and had even risked death in pursuing his responsibilities as a minister. We would be mistaken to read Paul's intent in presenting this catalogue of labors in any other way—as a number do, for example, in reading it as a confession of weakness - nor is his intention here to be confused with his intentions in presenting others of his catalogues. He is making a forceful claim to have publicly demonstrated in his work two other essential qualities of the minister. These are his fidelity to his summons and his dedication to the task. Thus the minister is not his own master but must work within his mandate.

There is a curious connection here with the way the ancient grammarians understood the etymology of their word for minister: in the two syllables of *dia-* and *kon-* they saw the ideas of 'through' and 'dust', finding these two ideas then totally appropriate to what was required of a *diakonos*, namely, that he raise the dust in the ardour and vigour of his efforts to complete his task. (And we notice in passing how immediately suggestive to them the word *diakonos* was of the swift courier, which is not, unfortunately, an element that survived into the modern perception of the word.) The labors of a minister signal his fidelity and his trustworthiness. Only a fool sweats over something he does not believe in.

Paul also reveals in his teaching and in his career that a Christian minister is not alone: no more is the church which he founds or leads. As a minister he is one among others who have been entrusted with the gospel. He is made part of the whole scheme of 'dispensation' or ministry (2 Corinthians 3.7-9) initiated in different ways by God. He works with others elected by God—one of Paul's typical designations of colleagues is 'co-workers'—in revealing the 'secret and hidden wisdom ... which God decreed before the ages for our glorification' (1 Corinthians 2.7). Within this mystery there is a communion of ministers working towards its manifestation. Paul insists that he is within this communion, instancing his connection with the founding tradition (1 Corinthians 15.1-5). Again, by definition, his Greek word for minister means, from his own phrase there, one who delivers what he has received. His view of the church as a body whose first functions are the teachings of the apostles and prophets (1 Corinthians 12.28) is his other way of presenting the communion of ministers, because the body in all its array and variety of members will only be one if the mystery from which it lives is one and the same in the variety of ministers and teachings.

From the communion of the ministers comes the communion of the churches. And one of the tasks of the minister is to bring his church into this communion and to sustain it there. In Luke's view of ministry we have seen this receiving expression in the form of a delegation between churches (Acts 11.29-30), and in this way too we will see Paul working very hard indeed to lead communities he had known to give practical expression to their unity of faith. His collection for Jerusalem is before anything else a ministry to the Spirit-filled fellowship of the churches, aiming to reveal, for all to see (2 Corinthians 8.21), 'the surpassing grace of God' (9.28) with which churches of varied nations abound.

A correlative of communion within fidelity to tradition is of course the minister's competence in the tradition. Again by definition, only the person competent to pass on a message can be the *diakonos*. The special character of the Christian tradition places a special demand on the minister. Because the tradition is not a body of knowledge but is a mystery given expression in the daily life of a body which is a church, the minister must first live from the mystery if he or she is to open it for others. Paul's writings betray this awareness and his special competence on every page. His awareness of the challenge which his place within the ministry has presented him with is such as to produce in him his 'anxiety for all the churches' (2 Corinthians 11.28).

Within this awareness we have the very origins of the title *minister/diakonos*. We have seen how intimately Paul binds it into his talk of the dispensation of God's gracious plans. The connection of the word with this phase of religious experience is not accidental but is part of the tradition of the word in the language he was using. Arising from such a tradition and further enriched by Paul's own usage, the title is not lightly used nor within a church can it be taken upon oneself. It is bestowed on those whom the church judges to be fitted for it. We have seen this in Luke's account of the selection of the Seven for ministry (Acts 6.1-6) and in his sketch of the delegation from Antioch (Acts 11.29). We see it too in what is Paul's last invocation of the title in the letter to the Colossians—if indeed the letter is Paul's, as I like to think it is. His reflections open in the timeless dimensions of 'the first-born of all creation' and descend to the time-enshrined gospel of which he, Paul, became a 'minister' (Colossians 1.23), a minister, he goes on at once to say, following the same movement from the other time to this, 'according to the divine office which was given to me for you, to make the word of God fully known, the mystery hidden for ages and generations but now made manifest to his saints' (1.25-26). This is the home of the language of ministry. Ministry in the church is of heaven.

5: Paul, Ministry, and Jerusalem

Ministry in the church is of heaven. The evidence for this in the language of the first Christians is so strong that one has to be surprised at the ease with which most churches began to lose touch with this legacy in the middle of the twentieth century. In chapter 2 we observed how the phenomenon expressed itself over recent decades in the virtually universal accord that one seemingly normative biblical passage—Ephesians 4.12—means the opposite to what churches had previously taken it to mean. To propose the traditional understanding now in ecumenical circles is to invite bemusement, and the proposal is likely to be disregarded as reactionary.

Switching ministry

The ease with which this switch of principles has been made, whereby all Christians are ministers, is to be attributed in a significant measure to a new way of understanding the language of ministry/*diakonia*. This is that the term designates a service that just about anybody can do. From what we have seen already, however, both Luke and Paul are reserving the use of ministry/*diakonia* to those in the church who carry an apostolic mandate, and in Paul's writings we observe powerful claims that what gives him his role among the churches is his heavenly mandate for ministry/*diakonia*. What we want to move on to observe now is how this heavenly ministry embodied itself in the activities of the churches at their beginnings.

The churches we will be looking at are those founded by Paul, because those are what we mainly have the information about, and in Paul's dealings with a number of them we find him speaking of himself and of the churches being involved in a ministry/*diakonia* very different from the one by which he had been mandated to found churches. And at this point, I think we can say, we begin to see how the modern switch in the understanding of ministry/*diakonia* became possible. Because the ministry Paul writes about here involves going to the help of the poor, people began to think that servicing people's needs was what made up ministry or *diakonia*. The thinking became that since some of our needs are spiritual and some are material, and since ministry is the action of servicing them, ministry has to be within the capacity of every sincere Christian. This line of thinking was forcefully endorsed by scholarly linguistic views which proposed that early Christians had chosen the *diakonia* words to express what they did in their churches precisely because they were words from the world of slaves and service.

Again, our impression so far of the words in the language of Luke and Paul is different from that. These were words that these writers—one of them, Luke, being a writer highly sensitive to the values and nuances of the Greek language—associated in a particular way with the rights and duties of people who had been mandated by God to proclaim a heavenly mystery. In naming an operation for the relief of the poor a ministry/*diakonia* these writers would not be saying that *diakonia* is service of the needy but that service of the needy comes within the mandate of *diakonia*. The heavenly ministry by which believers are brought under the gift of God invests believers with the earthly responsibility of sharing that gift with others. How this works out in the use of the language of ministry, and what the words actually mean in this connection, we will have the chance of observing in working through the story of the collection for Jerusalem.

The delegation to Jerusalem

Earlier we considered the delegation from the church in Antioch to the church in Jerusalem, noting how this was presented by Luke as a 'ministry/*diakonia*' (Acts 11.29; 12.25). On that occasion Paul was engaged with Barnabas as the junior of two delegates. In his own writings Paul has a lot to say about a later and more complex delegation to Jerusalem, one which he was mainly instrumental in planning but in which he wanted the churches themselves to take the leading part. These were the churches in Asia Minor and in northern and central Greece (Macedonia and Achaia, the latter including Corinth and Cenchreae) which he had founded, and his concept was of a splendid gift of money from these churches to the church in Jerusalem as their public attestation of a sense of fellowship with brothers and sisters in the Lord whom they had not actually met. Mounted as a delegation, the presentation of the gift would be a powerful statement by these remote churches of the vigour of the new life in the Spirit which had been opened to them through the ministry of Paul. It would assure the leaders in Jerusalem that different as the Greeks were from the Jewish followers of Jesus in the way they had responded to the new faith—not adopting the Jewish foodlaws, for example—there could be no real doubt that they were true followers.

Getting the delegation together, however, was going to present some problems, although these did not surface immediately. The churches in Macedonia, where he began, were well organised. Though poor, they had 'a wealth of liberality' ready for despatch (2 Corinthians 8.2), and they appointed two delegates to accompany Paul. These are called 'apostles of the churches, the glory of Christ' (8.23), which is an indication of how highly Paul esteemed their role and at what level he was pitching the delegation.

In Corinth things had not been running so smoothly. The church had been given instructions to make weekly savings for the gift so that there would be no last minute bottleneck (1 Corinthians 16.2). They were also instructed to have their delegates selected and furnished with letters of appointment (16.3). In regard to this part of Paul's instruction, readers of translations will notice that some translators want us to understand that these letters of introduction are to be written by Paul, but our discussion is aiming to show that Paul's concept of the ministry of the churches in this undertaking is such that writing letters of introduction himself for the delegates from Corinth is precisely what he does not want to be seen to be doing. About this side of the arrangements Paul was especially careful. He wanted each section of the delegation to appear clearly in Jerusalem as a representation from a particular Asian church at the same time as all the delegates were to be seen as representing one fellowship of churches.

In trying to get the Corinthians to see things this way, Paul knows he must avoid appearing to be intrusive, for while the idea of the delegation may have been his own he wants it to look like a work of the churches themselves; accordingly he indicates that he will go along only 'if it seems advisable' (16.4). In spite of his having shown this kind of consideration in his approaches to them, we notice that in writing about a year later he was still urging—indeed was reduced to cajoling—them at least to get the collection of money finished, and for this purpose sent Titus and the two Asian delegates to give them a lead (2 Corinthians 8.6 and 23).

For what is perhaps a third time he wrote to them betraying his continued anxiety about their readiness. And with this reference to a third letter, perhaps it is time for a comment on how many letters Paul did write on this matter. Views among scholars are very divided in fact on how many letters Paul actually wrote to the Corinthians and which ones were lost and how many fragments were put together to form 2 Corinthians, if indeed this 'letter' contains any fragments at all. For our purposes, however, these unresolved questions are not really important—even though I write as if letters were being written one after another— because what we are mainly looking for in any text that has survived is indications of why Paul estimated as ministry the churches' involvement in a delegation with an aid package for the poor in the church in Jerusalem.

At this point in the text (2 Corinthians 9.2) what we read is more cajoling: 'I know your keenness and I boast about it', but in going on to say that he is still going to send some organisers to hustle the Corinthians along Paul reveals the true level of his anxiety. Unashamedly he holds out to them how embarrassing it would be for all, not least for the church in Corinth, if the delegates from the northern churches should stop by to receive hospitality in Corinth before proceeding in the company of the Corinthian delegates only to find the Corinthians in a state of confusion and not ready to take part (9.3-5).

This being a possibility too distressing to contemplate, Paul seizes the rhetorical moment for a short but intense homily on the virtue of generosity. Here we strike what became our English saying, first formulated in William Tyndale's translation, 'God loves a cheerful giver' (9.7). But Paul does not indulge in mere platitudes—and this saying was already one in Paul's day—because he will proceed to press the Corinthians to weigh up just what it means for a local group to send a substantial gift by the hand of their own accredited delegates to a distant group of unknown foreigners on the grounds only that they share a common faith in the generosity of God.

Paul works towards his most persuasive idea only gradually. He moves from the 'cheerful giver' to some assurances that a generous God will make up for anything should their generosity run the Corinthians short (9.8-10). Even this, one is tempted to surmise, could have sounded pious and hollow when read aloud to an assembly of people whose daily lives depended on the hardnosed commercial bustle of Corinth. Paul's concluding reflection, however, would have been a challenge to all believers because it homed in on what such people experience in belief.

Believers then, like believers now, knew themselves most surely to be Christians in experiencing gratitude for 'the unsurpassing grace of God' which gives them fellowship in Christ and the Spirit (9.14). An awareness of God's graciousness is what keeps them in the communion both with God and with one another. Paul's own sense of gratitude was, of course, vibrant, and he seeks to evoke a response by striking this chord in those to whom he is writing. He puts it to them that if they enter fully into this charitable project there will be a remarkable effect in distant places. What will happen is that the believers in Jerusalem will not merely be grateful for the gift but will be moved to thank God for the generosity of the givers. Even more touchingly he asks the Corinthians to consider that these distant unknown people will be enlarged in heart at the realisation that foreigners have been moved to such generosity and to the exquisite niceties of a delegation as their confession of the gospel (9.13). On hearing this the Corinthians could only turn within themselves to see how real the gospel was for them. Was blessing such a part of their new life and experience that they should give material expression to it in favour of those unknown people who, they were told, shared with them the same blessing?

Subtle and intimate as this appeal by Paul clearly was, it was marked also by a poignancy which is easily lost to the modern reader. Today's readers are never going to know the exact history of Paul's dealings with this community of Christians founded by him in Corinth, and they may need to be reminded that long passages of Paul's correspondence with the community evidence aspects or perhaps phases of an intense conflict between the founder and the believers. We alluded to this conflict in chapter 4 when seeing Paul address himself to the Corinthian church as a minister.

Whatever of the details of his relationship—and it was all compacted into a period of four or five years—and at whatever stage of the conflict Paul wrote 2 Corinthians 9, in his appeal there for wholehearted community support for a demanding and complex community undertaking Paul had to cope both with the feelings which the conflict provoked in him and with the feelings which were either building up or were residual among the Corinthians. One can imagine Paul determining to use the challenge of a composite Asian deputation to Jerusalem as a means of repairing the damage which this purely local conflict had caused in the relationship with him but more especially in relationships among the Corinthian themselves.

A right and a wrong way

If the obscurity of the historical circumstances is one obstacle in the way of today's reader coming to appreciate what it meant for Paul to undertake a collection for the church in Jerusalem, a more awkward obstacle is the obscurity of some of the language used in our translations at certain critical points of Paul's references to it. More critical than anything else is the way the translations handle Paul's references to the collection as a ministry. The approach of the translations at this point has repercussions also in the translation of other elements of language in the context. Mainly, however, and most unfortunately, the translations fail to represent Paul's basic conception of the whole operation as a ministry.

In reading Luke's account of the delegation which the Christians of Antioch sent to Jerusalem, we encountered the term *diakonia* (Acts 11.29; 12.25). We found translators confusingly calling it in one passage a 'mission' and in another 'aid' or 'contribution'. Our own reading made it a sacred mission in both passages, and indeed this mission was itself a ministry. To appreciate how Paul is using the term, we can probably best compare two translations of the relevant passages. This will help to limit discussion, and should also clearly show what a difference it makes to our perception of what Paul is saying when we understand his ministerial terms as referring to a commission or a mission. In one column we will have phrases taken from the *Revised Standard Version* and in the other we will have my translation set within Paul's understanding of ministry. Translations of the same Greek phrases are parallel to one another in italics; translations of the Greek term for what we call ministry is in bold italics.

2 Corinthians 8.4
the churches of Macedonia
gave according to their means...
and beyond their means,
of their own free will,
begging us earnestly
for the favour

of taking part	*of taking part with us*
*in the **relief***	*in the **sacred mission***
of the saints	*to the blessed people*

2 Corinthians 8.19-20

he has been appointed	*he has been designated*
by the churches	*by the churches*
to travel with us	*as our fellow traveller to foreign parts*

in this gracious work	***in bearing** this gift*
which we are carrying on,	***under mandate***

for the glory of the Lord
and to show our good will.

We intend that no should
   blame us
about this liberal gift   *in this generous undertaking*
which we are administering   **that we have been**
                                      commissioned to carry out

2 Corinthians 9.1
Now it is superfluous for me
to write to you
about **the offering**   *about* **the sacred mission**
for the saints   *to the blessed people*

2 Corinthians 9.12-13
the **rendering**   **carrying out the sacred**
                                 mandate

of this service   *of this community work*
not only supplies
the wants of the saints
but also overflows
in many thanksgivings to God.
Under the test   *In the public reception*
of **this service**   *accorded to* **this sacred mission**
you [they*] will glorify God   *they will praise God*
by your obedience   *for your commitment*
in acknowledging the gospel   *to giving expression to the*
                                   gospel
(* Alternative translation in footnote)

Romans 15.25
At present, however,
I am going to Jerusalem
with aid   **on a mission**
for the saints   *from the blessed people*

Romans 15.31
[pray]
that **my service**   *that* **my sacred mission**
for Jerusalem   *to Jerusalem*
may be acceptable to the saints

In comparing these translations the reader is likely to be surprised at the degree of the variations, and not just the variations between the left and right hand columns but those also within the left hand column alone. After all, the words highlighted there are all intending to represent in English what Paul meant by his one Greek term for ministry or ministering (*diakonia*, the noun, and *diakonein*, the verb), and yet in the left column, in regard to the noun, we encounter ideas of *service in general*, of *service for people*, then of providing *relief*, of making an *offering* of a gift, and lastly of *rendering* a service; for the verb we are given *aiding* people, *carrying on* a task, and *administering* a gift. We know that in translation one word may often have to be put into English in different ways to meet its meaning in different contexts, but in the various translations we would normally discern an underlying linking notion, whereas here we cannot discern in English any connection between ideas like *administering* a responsibility and *aiding* someone. In the right hand column, on the other hand, we at once see a consistency in all Paul's references to the collection as a *ministry* or as a task needing to be *ministered*, even though we have needed to represent these in English by expressions like *sacred mission* and *carrying out a sacred mandate*.

Restoring ministry

This is not the place to explain why this approach to translating the words is correct. A detailed explanation has in fact been presented in my study of these words in the ancient Greek language, *Diakonia: Re-interpreting the Ancient Sources* (pp. 217-221). Just one or two points are worth repeating here. The first is a curious item of no great moment from a scholarly point of view but helpful in that it perhaps illustrates how the ancients could think of ministry/*diakonia* as a mission. In some manuscripts of Paul's letters to the Romans, including the prestigious *Codex Vaticanus*, at 15.31, instead of ministry/*diakonia* (translated above as 'my sacred mission'), we read the word *dorophoria*, which means 'carrying of gifts', and gives excellent sense at this point where Paul is expressing the hope that the gift of the collection will be well received in Jerusalem. In whatever way this variant word entered the tradition of the manuscripts—it entered into the Latin Vulgate Bible and from there is represented in the early English translation of Rheims (1582) as 'oblation'—the idea it expresses corresponds closely with the idea of a 'mission', especially as Paul's word *diakonia* implies here that his mission is one of getting something from one place to another.

A second point of language is rather more important. And it is this: to the eye of anyone who reads Paul's Greek the traditional translations are obviously struggling to come to grips with how he has expressed himself, and here and there they leave signs that they have just not been able to cope. Thus three times Paul uses the word *eis*, which most often in Greek we find ourselves understanding as *into* or *towards* because one of its common functions in language is to accompany words indicating movement towards a destination. In the right hand column above we see this *eis* represented as a mission *to* the people in Jerusalem; in the left hand column, however, there is no trace of this *to*, and an old-fashioned schoolmaster would not be very pleased to see the little word not only ignored but replaced by the word *for*, as in *service for* Jerusalem, *offering for* the saints, and by *of* as in *relief of* the saints. Interestingly, to go back to Romans 15.31, even the latest Vatican edition of the Vulgate Bible has replaced the age-old and totally unsatisfactory *obsequii mei oblatio* ('the oblation of my service', Rheims) with *ministerium meum pro Jerusalem* ('my ministry for Jerusalem'), and commits the same solecism.

A last point concerns the modern habit of seeing in these ministry/*diakonia* words in these passages a sign that Paul was thinking along lines of helping the believers in Jerusalem. Helping was, of course, one clear objective of the collection. But writers and translators frequently indicate a conviction that helping was what these particular words themselves signified. Thus at 2 Corinthians 8.4 we read in the *Good News* that the Macedonians are 'having a part in helping God's people in Judea'. The same idea is discernible in its translation at Romans 15.25, 'I am going to Jerusalem in the service of God's people there', and in the *Revised Standard Version* above, 'I am going to Jerusalem with aid for the saints.' In translations of this kind we lose touch completely with a basic notion of Paul's in regard to the collection.

We have been emphasising that what Paul organised was a mission or delegation. Now of its nature a delegation has a delegating authority behind it. In this case the authorities are several because each group of churches in Macedonia and Achaia has given a written mandate to its representatives on the journey. As against this arrangement, however, when we understand Paul as speaking of going to Jerusalem with aid for the saints—notice how the *Good News* emphasises just which saints are in question with its phrase 'God's people there', namely, in Jerusalem—we miss the idea of representation altogether. The saints Paul is talking about here are not the saints in Jerusalem at all—he mentions those in the next verse—but are the saints in the churches who have commissioned him and his companions to undertake the journey to Jerusalem. They are the saints in the churches of Macedonia and Achaia. The explanation of why this must be so is very simple. It is a point of standard Greek grammar (see again the book *Diakonia*, p. 327, note 9, where I illustrate the grammar) that in a phrase like 'ministering for the saints', which is what we have here, the saints have got to be the persons who give the mandate for the ministry. (The reader of English translations needs to be aware that 'for the saints' at Romans 15.31 translates a different Greek phrasing from that translated 'for the saints' at 2 Corinthians 9.1; in the latter instance the Greek phrase begins with the preposition *eis* referred to in the preceding paragraph, while in the former the Greek word for 'saints' stands without any preposition because it is simply the indirect object of the verb.)

Delegation as ministry

This has been a long discussion around grammatical, historical and literary aspects of Paul's letter writing in regard to the collection for Jerusalem. We were led into it because Paul refers to the collection in terms of ministry/*diakonia*. Further, because his references to the collection as ministry/*diakonia* are second only to his use of the terms in reference to his preaching ministry for frequency, pointedness, and nuance, we surely have something to learn from the phenomenon of the collection if we are seeking to appreciate the dimension and import of ministry for early Christians. Outside of these two major fields of ministry/ *diakonia*, namely his own and that of these churches of Macedonia and Achaia, Paul's only other references to ministry/*diakonia* are made in passing or without the depth of context which allows us to see the measure and weight of what he had in mind.

From his own experience as a minister/*diakonos* of the gospel, Paul knew that he was under a powerful call from God. A singular aspect of this call, as is evident in everything he wrote, was that the call not only commanded his whole life and gave direction to all his activities but also ushered him into a new phase of existence, which was his life in Christ. One is almost tempted to think of him experiencing the transition as more an entry into a new world than into a heightened religious awareness. Certainly his whole philosophic outlook was irrevocably altered, and this extended to his new view of the structure, power, and purpose of the universe as well as to the dislocation of the previous religious framework of his personal life. In other words, his role as minister/*diakonos* placed him in an immediate connection with the sphere of the divine and required him to extend the influence of that sphere among as many as might be open to the grace of its illumination. Those who believed had entered into it. His task thereafter, and the believers' own task within this new phase of existence, was to maintain the vital connection and to nurture the new vitality arising out of it.

Another dimension in his perception of the new world is that women and men are constituted as a society—one might say *at last* as a society because, finally in Christ, the creator's purpose was now realisable. One of his expressions of this social dimension was in the 'communion' of all believers with the Son (1 Corinthians 1.9), in the Spirit (2 Corinthians 13.13[14]), by the grace and illumination of faith (Philemon 6), from the common reception of the good news (Philippians 1.5). Within this communion life necessarily expressed itself in love and mutual accord (Philippians 2.1-2). This was the life within the sphere of God. Paul's most powerful literary representation of the communion of believers is, of course, in the living body of Christ that the churches are (1 Corinthians 12.12-27). His most forceful representation of it in his capacity as a pastor, however, was his orchestration of the Asian churches in the collection for the poor in the church of Jerusalem.

We underestimate the significance of this complex undertaking, which absorbed a great deal of Paul's time and energies, if we look on it merely as an act of charity, heroic in scale but a collection nonetheless. On first encountering the operation in these pages we saw that, in addition to its being a collection with a practical objective that we can easily appreciate, the project also had what might be called a political objective in that the Jewish church in Jerusalem would be encouraged to trust the orthodoxy or authenticity of these foreign groups of Christians who had been inspired to offer them generous assistance in material affairs. Beyond this objective, however, is another and more important one, which was that in extending practical charity in the demanding circumstances of travel over such distances and terrain in that area of the ancient world all those contributing in any way to the undertaking would be actively engaged in giving expression to the reality of their communion with one another, to the interdependence of the body of Christ. Paul even says that the Asians will 'make communion' in the interests of the poor (the *Bishops' Bible* of 1568 translates 'make a certaine common gathering for the poore saints', Romans 15.26), and proceeds to include this idea in going on to provide the rationale: if the Gentiles are 'in spiritual communion' with the Jews or 'hold the things of the spirit in common' with them they ought at least attend to their material needs (15.27).

For this sense of communion to find expression in any one church a certain number of things had to happen. For a household to put together a contribution, for example, a special savings program had to be introduced. Paul recommended a program of weekly savings. In whatever way a program was initiated, consideration had to be given to the means and the affordability, especially in communities which on Paul's indications were not well off (1 Corinthians 16.2; 2 Corinthians 8.2-3). This took a close consideration within each household not only of how much they could afford but of why they were entering into this difficult financial commitment from which they would receive nothing practical in return. Once the couriers set off with the money, that was the end of it.

We also notice that Paul mentions putting the savings aside on the first day of the week, and are reminded that when the Christians came together 'in assembly' or as a church (1 Corinthians 11.18) there would have been much to discuss about the practicalities of the community's offering. Someone had to know what the likely outcome of the contributions from households was likely to be and to co-ordinate the arrangements. Inequalities of financial standing would no doubt get an airing here and would have to be delicately handled. Schedules and accounting processes would have to be established. Untoward circumstances, like a bad season or a drop in trade or additional changes in the taxes or misfortunes affecting particular households, would have to be accommodated. And above all two things had always to be closely attended to. One was to maintain harmony within the community in an affair which could easily and for seeming good reason give rise to discord, complaints, and squabbles. How often would a spokesperson have uttered sentiments like those contained in Paul's encouragement to one of these northern communities: 'Let each of you look not only to his own interests, but also to the interests of others. Have this mind among yourselves, which you have in Christ Jesus...' (Philippians 2.4-5)?

The other main thing to be attended to was the maintaining of the high spiritual ideal on which Paul was basing the collection. For these Greeks, Jerusalem of the Jews was totally remote, and the idea of a spiritual communion across the islands and the sea and the intervening provinces of the Empire was strange and unreal. Only with a keen awareness of themselves as being 'in Christ', and of Christ as being a living bond, could they work together in their diverse congregations and aim to combine in one operation for the benefit of a distant people of whom they knew almost only that they too were a congregation of the Lord.

Against such ideals and within such constraints we are to weigh the fact that Paul consistently named the undertaking a ministry/*diakonia*. We can see now some of what went to the making of a ministry in the church from his point of view. Just as in his own ministry of preaching, this ministry too was constituted as ministry because it was *authorised*. Whereas his ministry was authorised by God, this ministry was authorised by the church. We have seen a glimpse of this in 1 Corinthians 16.3, where the church is to accredit its delegates, and in 2 Corinthians 8.18-19, where the famous unnamed preacher has been 'appointed by the churches'. Thus, what the church declares to be ministry is ministry. Here the ministry is a public activity, namely to travel to another church as a representative of one's own church in the delivery of a gift. Further, the gift-giving is not merely an act of generosity but an expression of the communal experience of faith; in this sense, the ministry is a proclamation and celebration of a shared faith, and one would like to have had the opportunity of reading in the letters of accreditation which these gift-bearers took with them the churches' varied expressions of their theology of communion in the Lord. We might note as well that, prominent in their local churches as one or other of these delegates in ministry were, their ministry on this occasion was temporary. The task done, they became one in membership again with their congregation.

Perhaps the strongest characteristic of their ministry was that it was a totally religious act arising out of a sense of Christian identity and, indeed, out of sensitivity to the demands of that identity. Ministry must conform to that pattern, which is first to be discerned within the needs and possibilities of a group of believers. It will also be tested against the discernment of other groups of believers, being authenticated in other words by its conformity to the common experience of faith, as part of the communion of all churches in the Spirit. The role of Paul, the founder of churches, was not determinative here. The churches had their own responsibility for this ministry, and yet they could only meet the responsibility by collaboration with each other.

Public, organised, accredited, and faith-filled, and whether it is the giving of a gift or the preaching of God's mystery, ministry enriched both those who established it and those to whom it was extended. As Paul said, it 'overflows in many thanksgivings to God' (2 Corinthians 9.11).

6: Paul's Colleagues

Paul's personal involvement in the activities of the Asian churches has meant that his surviving correspondence has left us occasional first-hand information about the style and purpose of the delegations as well as insights into his own estimation of them as religious ministry. For generations after him such visiting between churches would remain an important feature of their life. In the letters attributed to Ignatius of Antioch, for example, we have rich indications of this kind of activity. The official representations were by no means only for the purpose of providing assistance to a church known to be in some need but could be for any of the wide array of church matters. Very often the matter might be the introduction to one community of a respected member from another community, but it could also be to pay respects on the occasion of a celebration or of a grave loss, to gather for a conference, to join with others in experiencing a revered teacher, to exchange resources like liturgical or biblical texts or to pass them on. The churches were after all minority groups in the grip of their relatively new enthusiasm and were keenly aware of the value of sharing their experiences and hopes with others of like mind. All of this took a lot of energy, time, and financing, and occasionally we see Paul alluding to instances of it. About all that remains of the circumstances of these ventures, however, is the indication from him that these too, just like the delegation to Jerusalem, were in his eyes ministerial acts in the name of a particular church.

Stephanas

Thus it is only almost incidentally and among the personal notices at the end of Paul's first letter to the Corinthians that we hear of Stephanas having been involved with two others in a delegation to Paul. No translation a reader of this is likely to consult will, however, cast Stephanas, Fortunatus, and Archaicus in this role, and only rarely does a writer arrive at this assessment of the role of the three men. W. H. Ollrog, to whom we will be referring below, made this assessment very firmly in 1979, working largely from the context, which is interesting, and without the support of the linguistic background which is available to us. Instead of the idea of delegation, we generally encounter the idea of Stephanas having devoted himself 'to the service of the saints' or of some similar commitment the exact nature of which it is impossible to discern. Further, because in this instance the 'service' is our *diakonia*, which is the word so popular in our time for service to the needy, we will be informed commonly enough that Stephanas is recommended to the Corinthians as a typical leader because he has been helping other members of the community. This is doubly unfortunate because in the first place it gives the idea that leaders are best to be found among those who are doers of good services among the people—and the passage is cited by too many to this effect—and because in the second place we are thus deprived of learning just why Stephanas earned Paul's commendation.

The clue to what Stephanas has been at is in the phrase Paul applies to him and his household: 'they presented themselves for ministry/*diakonia* for the saints' (1 Corinthians 16.15). The ministry is the same as we have been reading about in the delegation to Jerusalem in the preceding chapter, that is, this household—especially in the person of its head, Stephanas—has been selected by the community to represent it in a mission related to the church's interests. On this occasion the church's interests are in its founder preacher, Paul, who is over the Aegean sea in Ephesus and with whom the church has already had some misunderstandings, as evidenced by the first few chapters of this letter, and is about to have some more of a graver kind, as evidenced by succeeding parts of Paul's correspondence with them.

This general situation of itself adds considerable substance to the purpose of a delegation between the church in Corinth and Paul in Ephesus. But more than that it also makes good sense of Paul's recommendation that such men make good leaders of churches. In making the recommendation Paul also alludes to another role being filled by the men, which is that they collaborated in the work of the gospel within their community; this is the standard meaning of Paul's terms 'fellow worker' and 'labourer' (verse 16). I have referred to three men as the group Paul has in mind, although we cannot be certain of the scope of the group he intends by 'the household of Stephanas'. He does mention only two other names in this connection, and they are names—one common Roman name meaning 'Lucky' and another undistinguished Greek name equivalent to something like 'Minnesotan' or 'Tasmanian'—well suited to the slaves or freedmen of an estate like that belonging to Stephanas. To visualise the group along such lines is possibly to be closer to the actualities than to think Paul is referring to Stephanas and his wife and children.

Our main interest on viewing this casual reference to further early Christian ministerial representatives is once again to evaluate this type of ministry. In our own age of such rapid development in the various technologies of telecommunication, the uses and skills of personal representation, especially by a small group for a larger group, are not easily appreciated, nor is the physical difficulty of the arrangements, as we have been reminded once or twice. A community, especially one like the Corinthian which has experienced some strain in its relationship with its founder, is going to enter into close discussion and consultation in its search for a suitable group of representatives. It is precisely in the sensitivities of personal exchange and debate in which the search for candidates engages the community that the value of its mandate for ministry lies. One must say this because only committed members of the community will engage themselves truly in the process, and only members committed to the values of the community—in this case the whole new spiritual world opened by the gospel as preached by Paul—will be able to arrive at an honestly and satisfactorily negotiated outcome. Wisdom, spiritual insight, practical acumen and a measured good will among all the participants are required to provide a community with a ministry suitable to its needs. In this case Paul's pleasure in the company of the nominated representatives, and his satisfaction in the ministry/*diakonia* which they performed in making the link between the church and the preacher, is plain to see; 'they refreshed my spirit,' he wrote (verse 18).

Phoebe

A more interesting, if disappointingly briefer, reference to such ministry is in relation to Phoebe (Romans 16.1). She being a woman, the reference may be said also to be more pertinent to talk of ministry in our times. Here again translations are usually of little value, and indeed too frequently now create a misleading image of Phoebe as a 'deaconess' of the church at Cenchreae. She is identified as 'deaconess'—even though no one is willing to describe what such a church officer might be at so early a stage of the development of officers in the churches—because Paul's note in recommendation of her uses the noun minister/*diakonos*, the same as is later used for the ordained deacon. (Writers often draw attention to the fact that this term is applying to a woman even though it is a Greek word ending in -*os*, which is a standard masculine ending; the word in fact is adjectival in form and like any other of its kind applies equally normally to women as to men, as is clear from at least the time that Aristophanes called the goddess Iris the messenger/*diakonos* of Zeus.)

The interest of Phoebe is revealed mainly in what we are able to read between the lines, but what we learn there endorses what we must infer from how Paul writes about her. Here is a 'sister' being 'commended', which alerts us to the striking fact that we have an individual Christian woman of one community—the word 'sister' tells us this much—being introduced by this singularly eminent missionary to another distant community. In addition we have the curious fact that the introduction is made by the missionary, who of course is Paul, before he himself has visited the community, which is that of Rome. In the first half of his list of greetings Paul does indicate that quite a number of people within the Roman households are known to him, these being converts or collaborators he had known in the East, some of them, like Prisca and Aquila, people who had been in exile there during Emperor Claudius' ban on Christians in Rome. The ban came into force 49 CE and seems to have become a dead letter some seven or eight years later. Others in the Roman church, however, would seem to be Christians from various households, perhaps leaders of churches, of whom Paul had been informed or of whose contribution to the church he had taken the trouble to become informed. Among these, for example, would be those named in verse 14. In other words Paul has constructed this list with care. It is not a perfunctory batch of greetings to a lot of people he did not know; we can be fairly sure of this if only because such a perfunctory list would be offensive to the un-named people among those he was planning soon to meet. He would seem rather to have directed these greetings to all those people whom he knew to be important in the running of the church or household churches in Rome. And at the head of the long list—his longest by far—he has written an introduction for a Greek woman by the name of Phoebe. Thus he would seem to have intended to establish a connection between this Greek woman and the leading Christians in Rome.

In his commendation of Phoebe we read of two outstanding qualifications. The first is that she is acting as a minister/*diakonos* of the church of Cenchreae. (I say 'acting as' because Paul runs an extra word in here which is crying out to be represented in translation somehow; literally 'being a minister', it introduces an unexpected emphasis to the title he attributes to Phoebe.) Cenchreae was the harbour city of Corinth, the important commercial centre, and housed another of the churches of Achaia that Paul had worked in. As minister/*diakonos* of this congregation on a journey to Rome, she has to be seen as travelling under this congregation's mandate. Again implied in such a situation is the process of selection and of assessment of objectives to which we referred in the case of Stephanas.

The second qualification of Phoebe is even more significant for an appreciation of why she is so prominent here, and in this I draw on a stimulating study by Robert Jewett, 'Paul, Phoebe, and the Spanish Mission', which he wrote for the volume dedicated in tribute to Howard Clark Kee, one of the significant recent scholars of the social setting of the early Christians (*The Social World of Formative Christianity and Judaism*, pp. 142-161). This qualification is as 'patroness' of Paul and of many others. This is not a light term, although the tradition of English translations has not helped us to appreciate it. As with minister/*diakonos*, which if it is not presented as 'deaconess' is presented as some innocuous 'servant', the Greek word for 'patroness' (*pro-statis*) has been translated in modern terms as 'being a good friend' and 'looking after people' or in the earlier language by 'suckered' (Tyndale, 1535) and 'hath given hospitalie' (*Geneva Bible*, 1560), which is to downgrade Paul's language and distort his purpose here. On such commendations we are led to believe Paul is asking the Roman Christians to give the visiting woman hospitality on the grounds that she has given good service in Cenchreae and deserves a good turn now that she is on the road herself. The word rather speaks of a woman of wealth who has used her wealth to support undertakings of the church in the persons of Paul and of 'many' others. With this background, and now in Rome under a mandate from her own church and probably also the bearer of Paul's letter there, she has a particular 'business'—so Tyndale and the next five early translations—to pursue. She is an accomplished businesswoman, and Paul wants her formally received so that she can get on with her task.

We may fairly assume that Paul had a hand in getting the church in Cenchreae to nominate and officially designate Phoebe as their minister/*diakonos*, and we surely know, although we must infer, that he has a keen interest in the success of what she is undertaking. We have also to infer that he expects all the leaders of the Roman households to facilitate her undertakings. This is the persuasive argument of Robert Jewett, and it neatly explains why Paul has drawn attention publicly to who these leading people are by including warm greetings to them in a letter which is to be read aloud around the various households. Paul is in fact drawing the Roman churches around Phoebe in support of the mission accorded to her by her church. Robert Jewett suggests that this mission is nothing less than getting arrangements in hand for Paul's own projected mission to Spain, announced in the preceding paragraphs of his letter (15.24,28).

What Paul's projected mission to Spain involved we need not go into, but the forward planning certainly included new kinds of logistical problems for Paul because there would be, for example, a switch of language from Greek to Latin, requiring new assistants for the missionary, and also a change of strategy in that Spain lacked the Jewish communities which so often had provided Paul with a start in his work. Not least were possible bureaucratic holdups as Roman officials hesitated over granting clearances for travel to new territories to a man whose reputation for being involved in public disturbances would possibly come ahead of him. Of course, at this stage, Paul was not to know that he would not come to Rome as a free man, although his request for prayers for his safety in Jerusalem (Romans 15.31) indicates his anxiety about the dangers there.

Some months ahead of his own anticipated arrival in Rome, and with the co-operation of the church in Cenchreae, Paul had in the imperial city an officially accredited representative of one of the established churches of Achaia, a wealthy woman of some social distinction. She would probably have presented herself in the first instance as the bearer of an impressive theological statement in the form of Paul's letter to the Romans, but her main and formidable task, once the introductions were over, was to marshall moral and organisational support for the next bold stage in the career of the great missionary. For the financial support she herself would continue to supply him Paul designated her 'patroness'; for her role as an officer sent out by her church to collaborate so closely with Paul, he named her for what they had made her, minister/*diakonos* of the church of Cenchreae.

Onesimus

While the case of Phoebe's involvement in ministry is full of interest, to see it for what it probably was we have had to draw on modern sociological studies as well as on the linguistic study which underlies this survey of early ministry. We are fortunate, therefore, still to possess in the one private letter of the many that Paul must have written an account of the circumstances in which Paul personally engaged another person for ministry. This was a most unlikely character from the other extreme of the social scale to Phoebe's, for it was Onesimus, the slave.

Perhaps we ought to remind ourselves at once that Onesimus was in a perilous situation. He had run away from his owner, who now had the right to punish him to any degree he chose, even with death. While there were many male slaves who attained at some stage to the lowly status of freedman, and a few who attained to some distinction in some walk of life, the vast majority of this majority of the inhabitants of Greece and Rome had nothing to strive for or to look forward to except perhaps an annual festival. A few years before Onesimus ran away—or perhaps he had not returned from some leave of absence (research and speculation about the legal and sociological circumstances of Onesimus have multiplied in recent years)—the Roman senate voted for the execution of four hundred slaves of one household as punishment for the one slave who had murdered the owner. Slaves counted for nothing.

The owner of Onesimus was the Christian Philemon, to whom Paul addressed the letter containing our information on the case. Philemon lived in Colossae, towards the south-west of Asia Minor, where a colleague of Paul's, Epaphras, had founded a church. Philemon was a leading member of this church, having a congregation centred on his house and acknowledged by Paul as a 'co-worker' or person involved in the work of the gospel (Philemon 1-2). Included in the address of the letter is the name of a woman, Apphia, presumably Philemon's wife, whom Paul knew to be a Christian because he greets her as 'sister'. A second man to whom the letter is addressed is greeted as 'fellow soldier', again a term referring to work in the campaign for the gospel. The man is Archippus, who at this time may have been responsible for the Christian community in nearby Laodicea (see Colossians 4.15-17); he may also have been the son of Philemon and Apphia. Thus Onesimus had been closely associated with Christians whose own lives had been intimately affected by involvement in responsibilities within a congregation.

Paul's whole letter, which is written from a prison—whether in Rome or Ephesus or even in Caesarea is debated—concerns his involvement with this slave. Paul is presumably aware of a legal obligation not to harbour a runaway slave and that for what time he does detain Onesimus he is to make financial compensation to the owner for the loss of the slave's services. Paul offers such compensation (18-19). He would seem to be writing to Philemon to have Onesimus peaceably reinstated in the household and, while this is generally agreed, it is curious to see how perplexed scholars can remain as to the precise intention of the letter. We are going to see that as the letter develops Paul insinuates a much larger purpose; indeed he writes to put a remarkable proposition to Philemon.

Onesimus is by now, on Paul's own very fond testimony, a close friend, his 'very heart' (12). He has also received Christian baptism at Paul's hand, this being the meaning of what Paul says about having become his father (10). Of themselves, these are striking developments in the life of a slave from such a Christian household, but we can be forgiven for wondering how Onesimus came to be in contact with Paul, of all people. Together in prison with Paul, however, is the founder of the church in Colossae, Epaphras (23), whom Onesimus undoubtedly knew from visits Epaphras would have made to the congregation at Philemon's house; in these circumstances we can imagine that a meeting with Paul could possibly have come about through Onesimus coming to Epaphras for advice or help. The close relationship which developed between Paul and Onesimus not only led Onesimus to baptism but revealed to Paul qualities in Onesimus which had never before perhaps been given play; they were those which Paul would have liked to use in extending his work for the gospel beyond his prison. This leads him to say to Philemon, immediately after providing the information that he has sent Onesimus back (12), 'I could have wished to hold him back here with me, so that,' he goes on (13), 'instead of you he might minister for me in the bonds of the gospel.'

Here again traditional translations are of little help to us when we want to determine what kind of ministry Paul was referring to in writing this. Translations are in fact generally clear in expressing the kind of ministry they have in mind, which is of the kind to be understood from the *Revised Standard Version*, 'that he might serve me on your behalf during my imprisonment for the gospel.' On this kind of reading Onesimus was to be Paul's prison slave, but the translation only arrives at it by some manhandling of the Greek. Principally this is in ignoring a link in the Greek phrasing which requires us to understand that it is the ministry, and not Paul, which is 'in the bonds of the gospel'.

In the light of this we have immediately to ask what kind of ministry Paul might really have had in mind, and we must certainly question whether he would have thought it fitting to speak of personal services in a gaol as services 'in the bonds of the gospel'. Those bonds for Paul were what bound him to his task of ministry, and in this sentence he is writing of his wish that they might be no less for Onesimus. Indeed, in the earlier phrase of this verse about wishing to 'hold back' Onesimus at his side, Paul uses a powerful word often associated in religious circles with binding a devotee to a commitment. What Paul is suggesting to Philemon, head of a household church, is that the runaway slave is now, although only newly a Christian, so deeply 'in the Lord' (16) or committed to the Christian community that he is capable of taking part in its ministry, in particular in the kind of ministry which Paul requires not only in his present circumstances, where he is deprived of freedom of movement, but so often also in his public ministry. This is the work of liaising with other churches and missionaries in the field, a work we often get glimpses of in references to men and women like Stephanas and Phoebe. With this in mind we see the force of Paul's introduction of the matter of the letter. In verse 8 he announces himself as 'an ambassador of Christ Jesus in chains' (often, but misleadingly, translated here as 'an old man'); that is, he is an elect representative to the peoples and cities of the empire who for the time being labours under a grave impediment. For now, in his chains, and for later, in his roving commission, he wants Onesimus to complement his activities.

One or two other aspects of Paul's approach in this letter are also of interest to the perception of ministry we can reach here. Paul knows that Philemon is involved in supporting the gospel in Colossae, and for this reason pays him the compliment of suggesting that Philemon himself would be pleased to perform the ministry Paul had in mind for Onesimus. This is the import of 'instead of you' in verse 13: Onesimus being a slave, whatever he does can be considered to have been done in the owner's name. Paul goes further than this, however, for he next suggests ever so obliquely that Philemon might see the value of releasing Onesimus to take up the same role once he returns to his household. 'Without knowing what you might think,' Paul writes in verse 14, 'I was unwilling to do anything.' He wished Philemon to arrive at this decision from the goodness of his Christian heart and without feeling that he had been forced into it by Paul (14). Indeed Paul suggests that a certain providence is to be seen in the unfortunate experience of Onesimus, because through it he returns to enrich the household of God with an additional 'brother' (16).

As the letter closes, Paul is bolder, suggesting that the situation between Philemon and himself is the reverse of what it might seem. Instead of Paul being in debt to Philemon by reason of having detained the slave, Philemon is indebted to Paul by reason of the new life he enjoys in the Christian community (19). In the opening paragraph of the letter (4-7), Paul has already paid a gracious tribute to Philemon's lively role in the community, and we are left to understand that all debts will be settled if Philemon gives Paul some 'profit in the Lord' (20) by releasing Onesimus for ministry. The final twist is Paul saying he is confident of Philemon's acquiescence, writing that he knows Philemon will do even more than Paul has suggested, this being no doubt to give Onesimus his freedom (21). He wants a bedroom ready for a stay with Philemon on the release he is expecting from prison (22), and then surely he will learn whether Philemon has made Onesimus available as a colleague in ministry.

If we compare the ministry Paul has in mind for Onesimus with that of Phoebe, the contrast is great. On the one hand is a wealthy woman of high standing in the community whom the church is privileged to be able to commission for a daring undertaking which aims to take the gospel beyond further seas to Spain, a woman furthermore with the entrepreneurial and diplomatic skills to raise community support in Rome and to deal with officials there. On the other hand is a common slave whose only grace is to have been touched by the Lord but in whom Paul has discerned qualities useful in the service of the gospel. For this reason Paul has decided to put the call of ministry upon Onesimus. This ministry cannot be at the level of Phoebe's, but is a ministry which can grow and in which the slave can grow. Importantly, since in the case of a slave it is not a ministry which Paul is himself free to impose, he must ask the slave's owner to recognize it and allow arrangements to be made.

Once Onesimus returns to the household he will, of course, be a member of the congregation there, and the question of his ministry will become a public matter. In fact Paul almost ensured that it would by including a warm commendation of Onesimus in the public letter to the congregation at Colossae which Tychicus was to deliver along with the private letter to Philemon. A 'faithful and beloved brother'—all strong, new Christian commendations—is how Paul referred to the runaway slave of the household now once more in their midst but now on an equal footing with them 'in Christ' (Colossians 4.7). Philemon, accordingly, has a lot to come to terms with, and his fellow Christians, Onesimus himself not least among them, will perhaps be drawn into evaluating the situation which has been orchestrated by Paul. In his private words to Philemon, Paul had already reminded the leader of the style in which affairs of the community were to be handled: a 'communion in faith' was to be effectively expressed in the actual experience of all the good they possess in Christ (6). Naturally, something affecting their life together so closely as the calling to ministry of their leader's slave present among them must have fallen squarely within that experience of communion. And certainly, in Paul's approach to the slave's owner in this letter, we see Paul moving from one persuasive position to another until he seems to have left Philemon no room to do anything other than to release Onesimus to take up a ministerial role.

Is the fact that the letter has survived a sign that Paul's objective was achieved and that Onesimus did ministerial work? Outside of this letter and of the commendation in the letter to the Colossians there is no sign of him in the earliest literary remains of the Christians. The Onesimus addressed some fifty years later as bishop of Ephesus by Ignatius of Antioch in his letter to the church there is perhaps unlikely, as the great scholar J. B. Lightfoot felt last century, to be the same person, and yet a more recent scholar of the standing of John Knox has felt that this was indeed the same man. More than that, he would be the man responsible for publishing the collected letters of Paul. No wonder the private letter which brought him his freedom, bequeathed to him by Philemon, is included in the collection. And to complement the collection Onesimus would have written, under Paul's name, the magisterial treatise on church and ministry which we call the letter to the Ephesians. If the case were so, as F. F. Bruce has sympathetically written, 'Paul accomplished something more wonderful than he could have realised the day he won Onesimus to faith in Christ!' (*The Epistles to the Colossians, to Philemon, and to the Ephesians,* p. 202). Beyond such reconstructions—and they are not merely fanciful—of the involvements of these personalities in the obscure history of their times, there are only late legends about Onesimus being a bishop in Beroea, near Paul's Philippi in Macedonia, of his travels to Spain, where Paul had planned to begin a missionary venture, and of martyrdom in Pozzuoli, the ancient Puteoli beside Naples and port of Rome, where Paul had disembarked as a prisoner on his progress to that city.

Ministerial assignments

Onesimus was to be just one more of a long-standing team working in ministry with Paul. In Paul's letters and in the Acts of Luke we run up against many passing references to people who were in this team from time to time or in one place or another, and we pick up also what are usually minor indicators of how its members went about their ministry. Paul's method in working like this has been the object of much scholarly attention in latter years, and the field of investigation is now a large one. Just on the numbers of people involved, for example, the German scholar Wolf-Henning Ollrog has compiled a dossier for each of the seventy or eighty men and women whose names are known from the sources. Informative stories about a dozen of the more familiar characters among these—Timothy, Luke, Priscilla, Apollos, Titus, Mark and others—have been put together, and carefully situated in what can be fairly confidently known of Paul's own story and style, by F. F. Bruce in *The Pauline Circle*.

Beyond that kind of information, however, we still have a lot to discover and to build into the picture of missionary activity in the first years of the Christian communities. One area is the language that was in circulation to designate roles and activities.

Huge amounts of information about who said what and in what terms in the ancient world have been collected in multi-volume dictionaries since the seventeenth century, and laboriously updated to the nineteenth and then to the twentieth century, but when we come down to what a particular writer had in mind with the use of a particular expression in the course of a discussion in one time and place we are very often still left with a delicate work of interpretation on our hands.

Of terms used in relation to Paul's mission, for example, the one springing immediately to mind for most people is possibly *apostle*, and yet rather more revealing of what the mission was in the complexity of its unfolding is a set of words much neglected in earlier scholarship which largely relate to what we would perhaps think of as being an *employee* but for the ancients related to the world of *servanthood*. This is an area of which we have no experience today and hence poorer chances of understanding in another culture from another time. And yet to come to understand the mission of the early Christians, and to assess what values that historical experience might hold for ministry in churches today, we find ourselves confronted with the following kind of conundrum. In four passages to do with ministerial activity in Paul's experience we can read in one of our translations the same word 'servant[s]' (1 Corinthians 3.5; 4.1; Romans 1.1; Philippians 2.25), and yet in each of these passages Paul used a different Greek word, each with its colour, weight, and significance for what he was saying. Other terms relating to *work* and to *soldiering* are also common and are revealing of particular aspects of what missionary activity was really about.

To cope with all that sort of information is not our task here, and in fact the German writer just mentioned, W.-H. Ollrog, did a very helpful thing over ten years ago in bringing a great deal of it together in a book called *Paul and his Co-Workers* (*Paulus und seine Mitarbeiter*). Fortunately our task is narrower than that, for we are seeking to draw out insights only from that part of the mission which our contemporaries call ministry and the ancients called *diakonia*. Our agenda has actually been set by the contemporary fascination with ministry as *diakonia* and, if the picture of the ancient *diakonia* that is emerging from our sketch does not correspond with contemporary estimates, there is all the more value for us in fixing the ancient perception in the ancient focus.

Thus, in the instance of Onesimus, we miss entirely an important initiative on Paul's part in regard to ministry if we follow the translations and conclude that all Paul was looking for was someone else's slave to look after him. By the same process we have learnt that Phoebe was not some mysterious deaconess of the church of Cenchreae or a singularly kind lady of that community but a highly competent woman on an enterprising mission which was considered to be ministry by those who commissioned her. And Stephanas, so often portrayed as a devoted social worker who for his services was recommended for advancement by Paul, is similarly a man working with his colleagues under the constraints of a ministry authorised by his community. In each of these cases the ministry in view is an assignment beyond the circle in which it originates. Onesimus is to liaise for Paul with other individuals and communities, Phoebe is arriving from Cenchreae to set up a support system for a major new initiative by Paul, and Stephanas and his colleagues have travelled from Corinth to a consultation with Paul in Ephesus.

The role envisaged by Paul for Onesimus is of the kind Luke has presented Timothy and Erastus filling (Acts 19.22), although here we do not have information on the exact purpose of their mission. The same type of role is intended for Mark at 2 Timothy 4.11, where we read in the *Revised Standard Version* 'he is very useful in serving me' but in Tyndale (1535), 'he is necessary unto me, for to minister', which at least gets the balance of the Greek sentence right and makes it that much easier for us to understand that the writer was thinking of Mark's ministry as going out on particular missions. We have a vivid glimpse of one such mission, perhaps, in the thankless journey of Onesiphorus to Rome to find Paul and give him support in prison; the writer says that Onesiphorus had 'ministered many times' in Ephesus (2 Timothy 1.18) and, while we cannot be sure of this, is possibly alluding to other journeys undertaken in the name of a missionary like Paul or on a commission from his community.

The sustaining ministry

We are not to underestimate the importance of these linkages between ancient churches and between preachers and remote communities. In calling the work of linkage ministry Paul and other ancient writers were identifying the work as integral to the mission and as enriching for the new kind of life the communities were attempting. The bonding which a personal representative of a church or a preacher could effect was a source of encouragement and an occasion of joy. Perhaps at times a minister's task was to issue a warning or inculcate a correction, although no such role is recorded as ministry. In Tychicus, 'faithful minister/*diakonos*' (Colossians 4.7, and compare the almost identical notice at Ephesians 6.21), we do see an instance of the ministry of liaison including a ministry of preaching. Sent to present the letter to the church in Colossae and to give a personal edge to the rapport between the writer of the letter and its recipients, he was also under instructions to do the job of a visiting preacher and lift the hearts of the congregation with some encouraging addresses.

The same writer, who is someone very close to Paul if it is not Paul himself, has already demonstrated in the language he used of Paul at Colossians 1.23 that he knows the scope and power of the ministry of the word in the minister/*diakonos*. We considered the passage in surveying the ministry of Paul himself. The purveying of the mystery presented here (1.13-20) is the ministry/*diakonia* which Paul defended as his prerogative before the Corinthians. It is from the reception of this mystery, by entry into it, that a church begins and grows, and the essential ministry is to proclaim it so that it is revealed. In his first paragraph of this letter the writer recognises Epaphras as one who has been a minister/*diakonos* with this capacity (1.7): 'faithful minister/*diakonos* of Christ on our behalf' who has brought to the Colossians 'the word of truth, the gospel' (verse 5). The designation here is worth taking note of. Epaphras has been commissioned by Paul or the writer ('on our behalf') and thereby has been commissioned as a 'minister of Christ'. (A noticeably weaker reading says 'on your behalf'; a copyist was perhaps distracted by verse 8 to think of Epaphras as a liaison between

Colossae and Paul.) Colossians concludes with a curt direction
to Archippus, of the household of Philemon and possibly leader
of the church in Laodicea, to fulfil his ministry/*diakonia* (4.17):
we can only say that this sounds like the ministry of leading and
sustaining a church, but we cannot be specific.

Timothy

If it was Paul who called himself 'a minister according to the
divine office' at Colossians 1.23, this would have been the last
time he used the word in writings that have come down to us.
The phrase resonates with all the values and mirrors all the
perspectives that ministry in the church contained for Paul. This
holds even if the writing, as probably most suspect, is from some
other under Paul's name. That too would show, as do other later
instances of the title, that the terminology was not just Paul's own
but part of the church's. We will follow the terminology through
on the little evidence that survives from those times in the later
letters to the churches. Never again, however, will rights to the
title of 'minister' be debated as Paul debated them in his Corinthians letters. That time of rivalry was passing—or perhaps more
accurately the rivalries that persisted or came to disturb the
churches did not generate accounts of this kind of debate in the
surviving documents. The documents that do survive are evidenc-
ing more an awareness that the church must conserve the heavenly mystery than that the mystery is newly made manifest. This
kind of more settled experience of the mystery will mean that the
minister/*diakonos*, the one with the message from heaven, will
give way to the officers in the church responsible for maintaining
the message and keeping it as a living tradition. Nonetheless, we
can see from Paul's own practice, as we have already seen in
Luke's portrayal of how the Twelve extended ministry to the
Seven (Acts 5.42-6.7), that a minister/*diakonos* can bring others
within his ministry/*diakonia.*

Although Paul resisted the right of those opposed to his
ministry to call themselves 'ministers of Christ' (2 Corinthians
11.23), he did not reserve the title to himself. The spread of the
gospel requires more than one minister. We have already seen

how he presented Apollos to the Corinthians as a 'minister' on an equal footing with himself (1 Corinthians 3.5). And in fact what is possibly his first recorded use of the term is in a tribute to one of his colleagues, Timothy. This is in his first letter, to the Thessalonians, but because there is some doubt as to what words he originally penned at this point, we need to look at differences of phrasing in the different manuscripts of this letter.

Some readers might wonder why a scholarly question like the original state of the text in the light of available evidence from the surviving manuscripts should be raised in a simple exposition like the present one. The reason is that in this case we encounter the factors which have influenced the modern editors in adopting the reading that they do, and in the process we learn a little more about the character and significance of our Greek word for 'minister'. Let us see what options the manuscripts provide the editors with when they come to choose among the different phrases alluding to Timothy. In a simplified form the different phrases can be displayed as follows (1 Thessalonians 3.2):

[a]   our brother and God's co-worker in the gospel of Christ
[b]   our brother and co-worker in the gospel of Christ
[c]   our brother and minister in the gospel of Christ
[d]   our brother and God's minister in the gospel of Christ
[e]   our brother and God's minister and our co-worker in the gospel of Christ

From the intermingling of these phrases, which takes our minds back to the centuries before printed books brought a large degree of consistency into the way we preserve what people wrote, we can see that copyists have had to choose between 'co-worker [of God]' and 'minister [of God]', and we probably assume that the copyist responsible for the phrases in [e] was playing safe by including both. In trying to determine in such cases what the author originally wrote, scholars generally draw upon their knowledge of the reliability of the different manuscripts. In this case phrases with 'co-worker' and phrases with 'minister' are spread fairly evenly around what are considered to be the more reliable manuscripts—the balance tipping on this score probably towards 'minister'—so that scholars have chosen to bring other considerations into play.

One of their considerations has been how the early copyists would have reacted to reading Paul praising Timothy in the highest terms, and some have concluded that some copyists may have felt such high praise to be out of place because it could detract from Paul's unique eminence as an apostle in the minds of the ordinary people of the congregation. Such thinking would have led these copyists to substitute for the high-sounding phrase one of a lesser quality. Now in this instance some modern scholars have felt that the highest-sounding phrase is 'God's co-worker'; on the other hand, they understand the term 'minister/*diakonos*' to be a lowly designation deriving from the language of servants and slaves. On these grounds, they suggest, the term 'minister' crept into many manuscripts but ought not to be recognised as part of what Paul originally wrote about Timothy.

In contrast with this line of thinking, the qualities we have seen attaching to the term 'minister' by reason of what Paul wrote in 1 and 2 Corinthians make the phrase 'a minister [of God] in the gospel of Christ' the highest commendation of Timothy which Paul could have made. And if we tack the modern line of argument on to that, we would be excused for thinking that 'minister' is what Paul would have written.

The instance would be most interesting because not only would it be the first occurrence of the famous word in Christian writings but it would evidence Paul using the word at the beginning of his writing career as a Christian in just the kind of way a non-Christian writer might do. And he would be using it without being provoked into it by the kind of challenges which soon faced him in Corinth and which incited him to weave the word into his defence with considered and considerable rhetorical skill. If we let the term stand in his text, it connects Timothy with the word of the gospel, points to his role of 'establishing' the Thessalonians in faith and of 'exhorting' them to live in it, and, since it occurs in a commendation of the person who has been sent among the Thessalonians for such purposes, lends that person all the authority he might require for such tasks. These are some of the qualities evident too in the minister that Paul revealed himself to be, as we have seen.

Later tradition about Timothy maintained this link with Paul's term for ministry. The first letter to Timothy, purporting to come from Paul, has the apostle thanking the Lord for having 'appointed me to ministry' (1 Timothy 1.12) and then, in its instruction to Timothy, holds out the way to being 'a good minister of Christ Jesus, nourished on the words of the faith and of the good doctrine' (4.6). This is the minister of the later church, linked still in his role with the word but a word now more clearly and fully determined by a lengthy tradition within the church. The authority of this minister is no less firmly implied than in the earlier times but is arising from the degree of the minister's fidelity to the tradition rather than from the minister's immediate commissioning by the Lord, as with Paul and Luke's Twelve. An exhortation in similar vein occurs in 2 Timothy, leading up to the concluding phrase, 'fulfil your ministry' (2 Timothy 4.5). Luke too associates Timothy with ministry in a phrase translated in the *Revised Standard Version* 'two of his [Paul's] helpers' (Acts 19.22) but better translated 'two of those who went away on ministerial assignments at Paul's behest'.

7: Greek Ministries

Why did early Christians use the name ministry/*diakonia* for the roles of preaching and of inter-church delegation and for a number of other functions within the community? To this question there is a widely accredited contemporary answer, and then there is the different answer which this chapter will provide. Both answers glow with the romance of language, the contemporary one sparkling with an almost irresistible appeal. Let us first look briefly at this. It is an answer with which many readers will be familiar.

The servant myth

In introducing chapter 5 we recalled that people generally think of *diakonia* as being especially expressive of service to the needy and as originating in the ancient Greek vocabulary for slavery. Prior to this century virtually no one drew attention to such characteristics of this word or of its cognates. Perhaps the only thing about the words which attracted occasional comment was that, while they were almost always translated into English by words like *ministry* and *minister,* in two passages of the New Testament and in quite a lot of passages in other early Christian writings the words appear in English as *diaconate* and *deacon* instead of as *ministry* and *minister.* Something similar happened in other European languages. We will not delay on this seeming inconsistency of translation, and only remark on it to indicate the level of interest these words attracted in previous periods of scholarship.

In modern times interest in the words sharpened noticeably when a story began to emerge explaining why it was that the words came to prominence among the early Christians. How prominent this was we can infer from the way Luke named the basic churchly activity 'ministry/*diakonia* of the word' (Acts 6.4). The story goes like this. Early disciples were particularly responsive to the fact that the Lord Jesus had lived, taught, and died in lowly and even degrading circumstances, and in seeking to represent this leading characteristic of their master in their own code of behaviour and in their way of associating together as a congregation or church they looked around for a suitable set of words to adopt. They did not have to look far because the best words were already part of the language of their central rite. The rite, of course, was their eucharistic meal, where they celebrated among other things the memory of the master who said he was among them 'as one who serves/*diakonon*' (Luke 22.27).

With this tradition about Jesus as a beginning, the story of the words soon developed along broader lines. If the master chose to be seen as a servant, the leaders of the congregations had to follow. As a point of language within their organizations this meant that they could not use the normal Greek terms for masters and rulers because these implied dignity and power. Hence their choice of the *diakonia* words. The background of these words, so the story is careful to explain, was where the story about Jesus at the supper put them. They were words for the slaves who waited at tables, and they were part of the everyday language of the Greek world, which was so full of slaves of various kinds. Gradually the words were used to apply to more and more of the life of the Christian community and were constantly signalling to Christians that whatever they did was to be done in the spirit of the Lord who served others (compare, as always, Mark 10.45).

When modern writers trace this kind of story of the words, they will often remark on how the meanings of the ordinary Greek word 'developed', as they tend to say, under the impact of this experience within early Christian communities. They may comment too on how innovative and, indeed, how creative the early Christians were in developing this part of their terminology. The story is represented in many influential books and encyclopedias published around the 1960s, some of them still in use as text books in theological colleges, like Eduard Schweizer's *Church Order in the New Testament* and Hans Küng's *The Church*.

The theological student—and today this student is not just the young man or woman who is a candidate for ordination but is as likely to be a mature adult seeking to arrive at a renewed appreciation of his or her position in the church—who is following a course on ministry in the church will be directed at some stage to the second of the twelve volumes of Kittel's *Theological Dictionary of the New Testament* for the purpose of reading the article about *diakonia* and its cognates by H. W. Beyer. This study appeared in German in 1935 and in English in 1964, and for our purposes can be considered the scholarly prop on which the contemporary view of ministry/*diakonia* leans. It presents a lot of information on occurrences of the words in pre-Christian Greek literature before moving into an account of the words in the New Testament. The lines of development are as just sketched here, and one comes away with a view of *diakonia* as expressing 'the full sense of active Christian love for the neighbour and as ... a mark of true discipleship of Jesus.'

An illustration of how far this view has travelled since 1935, and at what depth it is still working in the churches, is in the report which the General Secretary of the Central Committee of the World Council of Churches made on the eve of the World Council's Eighth Assembly in Canberra, 1991. The second of three sections of the report is devoted to a vigorous discussion of the churches' responsibility for what is called diakonia—no italics, just another English word—and described as 'a manifestation of practical love for human beings who are in need' as well as being held up as 'constitutive of our identity as the church' (*The Ecumenical Review*, 42[1990], 340-341). There is nothing new in this. The fashion was established in the World Council's policies in the 1950s, and it derives from the word studies of two or three scholars and the uncritical reception of their conclusions by writers on church and ministry.

In this chapter called 'Greek Ministries' we will sample what classical and Hellenistic Greek literature evidence about *diakonia*. This will reveal to us part of the real story of how early Christians came to designate their leading religious functions as *diakonia*. The story is not as romantic as the one we have just briefly told but is true to the ways of language. We will begin with an incident from the life of one of the great storytellers of those times.

The prophet who lived in an emperor's house

Jotapata was one of half a dozen important towns of Galilee which a well-to-do thirty-year-old Jew known to us as the historian Flavius Josephus was commissioned to defend against attack by the Roman army during the revolt of the Jews against the Romans in 67 CE. The Roman army was under the command of Vespasian, who, in an unsettled period in the succession of power in Rome, was to be proclaimed emperor by the army in the Middle East in 69 and would be emperor for ten years. The lives of these two men were intimately connected in almost unbelievable circumstances.

After a siege lasting 47 days, Vespasian subdued Jotapata—at the expense, Josephus records, of the lives of 40,000 inhabitants —and two days later captured Josephus, who was hiding in a cave. Imprisoned, Josephus was to be sent for display to Emperor Nero but instead, within two years, had become an associate of Titus, Vespasian's successor as Roman military commander in Judaea, during the long drawn-out siege of Jerusalem, and on the completion of the demolition of that city accompanied the victorious general to Rome to spend the rest of his days living in a villa that had been the home of Emperor Vespasian.

For an explanation of this remarkable change in the fortunes of Josephus we have to rely on his own writings. While scholars debate both the reliability of his account and the motives inspiring his portrayal of this critical period of Jewish history, there is no denying the drama of the story or the literary skill of the narrator. From our point of view the interest is in how Josephus' fortunes changed because he claimed to be a minister/*diakonos* of God.

Josephus had not been hiding alone from the Romans in the cave by Jotapata. With him were no less than forty other fugitives. They were discovered, and Vespasian sent for Josephus to surrender. This his companions would not allow for a Jewish general, and instructed him either to suicide or to receive execution from them. Josephus countered by making a speech on the immorality of suicide, and this so inflamed the group that they attacked him. Surviving this, Josephus next proposed that they draw lots by which one would kill another and thus they might all escape the taint of suicide. As Josephus tells it, the fugitives died until he and one other were left alone, whom he then persuaded, for the best of ethical reasons, not to proceed any further. Surrendering, he was taken to Vespasian.

Josephus emerges from this stratagem not quite the coward as at first appears because built into the tense scene, but not mentioned in our summary, is an account of how at this moment he came to an awareness that he had an as yet unfulfilled role to play before the Romans in the name of the Jewish God and must therefore survive. The awareness broke upon him during a parley with the Roman representative sent to press for his surrender and as the threatening shouts of the crowd waiting outside filled the cave. His words are carefully chosen and, as we can sense even from the English translation which follows, are rhetorically balanced to achieve an imposing effect. They are from his *Jewish Wars* 3.351-354:

> Suddenly there came back into his mind those nightly dreams in which God had foretold to him the impending fate of the Jews and the destinies of the Roman sovereigns. He was an interpreter of dreams and skilled in divining the meaning of ambiguous utterances of the Deity; a priest himself and of priestly descent, he was not ignorant of the prophecies in the sacred books. At that hour he was inspired to read their meaning, and, recalling the dreadful images of his recent dreams, he offered up a silent prayer to God. 'Since it pleases thee, who didst create the Jewish nation, to break thy work, since fortune has wholly passed to the Romans, and since thou hast made choice of my spirit to announce the things that are to come, I willingly surrender to the Romans and consent to live; but I take thee to witness that I go, not as a traitor, but as thy minister [*diakonos*].'

The list of Josephus' credentials here is impressive. As well as being a priest from a line of priests, and thus in the eyes of his readers set apart to mediate between God and mortals, he was also skilled in divination and thus enjoyed access to God's 'ambiguous utterances' in dreams. Beyond that, he was versed in the Jewish scriptures and, at that moment, had arrived at the perception of their ultimate prophetic import. Compounded with this professional knowledge was the ominous realization, born of communing with God in dreams, about the hidden fortunes of Jews and the Empire. The most astonishing aspect of this apologia appears in the prayer where he expresses the belief that God's work with the people of the ancient covenant was at an end. In such a momentous context, choosing his words carefully, and leaving the word of his choice to the very end of his elaborate Greek period, Josephus nominates himself as the minister/*diakonos* of God who must not die before he has delivered God's message to the Romans.

Josephus takes his role as God's minister/*diakonos* more deeply still into his history of the times. On hearing that he is to be sent to Emperor Nero, he requests an audience with Vespasian, and in the presence of his son Titus and two of Titus' friends addresses him boldly (3.400):

> 'You imagine, Vespasian, that in the person of Josephus you have taken a mere captive; but I come to you as a messenger of greater destinies. Had I not been sent on this errand by God, I knew the law of the Jews and how it becomes a general to die.'

For 'messenger' here Josephus writes *aggelos* instead of *diakonos*, and in his address goes on to announce, while Nero is still emperor and the complex historical events of his succession are yet to unfold,

> 'You will be Caesar, Vespasian, you will be emperor, you and your son here. Bind me then yet more securely in chains and keep me for yourself; for you, Caesar, are master not of me only, but of land and sea and the whole

human race. For myself I ask to be punished by stricter custody, if I have dared to trifle with the words of God.'

The immediate impact of this daring prophecy was not great. Vespasian tended to discount it as a piece of special pleading, but at least Josephus was not sent to Rome, and for two years was a prisoner of war in Caesarea under not particularly arduous conditions. He took a second wife, a fellow Jewish prisoner. When, however, the army in Caesarea proclaimed Vespasian emperor in 69, Josephus reports that Vespasian began to reflect on the providence which had brought him to this state and was reminded of the prophetic words of the Jewish general. On finding that Josephus was still in chains, he called a gathering of officers and friends to remind them also of 'the divine prophecies' of this one-time military opponent, and he declared (4.626):

> 'It is disgraceful that the one who foretold my attainment of power and was the minister [*diakonos*] of God's voice should still rank as a prisoner of war or endure the lot of a bound criminal.'

We have seen what Josephus' subsequent career and rewards were: he would be the historian of the conflict between Rome and his own people, and favourite of emperors. But while scholars continue to discuss the accuracy of this picture of himself—a comprehensive survey is by Per Bilde, *Flavius Josephus between Jerusalem and Rome*—we can be sure of the words he used and of the value he attached to them. In this almost melodramatic turnaround in his personal fortunes, the pivot is his realisation that he is a spokesman for God. What God requires him to announce is a secret of the future and a mystery of greater proportion than any prior prophet of his race had comprehended. It was the end, as he wrote, of God's 'work' for his chosen nation. At the very moment the prophet discovers his calling and accepts it in prayer before God, and again at the moment the emperor acknowledges the role of the prophet, Josephus writes the word 'minister/*diakonos*'. As a writer, he could not be more emphatic in the attention he is drawing to the significance of this designation. Other terms were to hand; one of them he used in presenting himself to Vespasian at Jotapata (messenger/*aggelos*), but for the climactic moments in his dramatic account of the incident which changed his life Josephus selected *diakonos*. His choice speaks to us not only of the place the word held in his own literary thesaurus but also of the place he knew it held in the esteem of his readers.

The world's greatest storyteller

In the next pages we will draw on other passages from ancient literature which illustrate in a significant way the uses writers made of the word *diakonia* or its cognates for the purpose of expressing ideas about delivering messages, especially messages which came from another world. From there we will move to passages illustrating the authority of the minister/*diakonos*, and conclude by examining what it meant to be a minister/*diakonos* at a banquet. In all of this we will take note as well of how ancient writers found these words suggestive of religious connotations which they wished to raise.

The first story we will let speak for itself. It is based on the life of Aesop, which itself lends it a particular prestige. The life was written in the first century (*Vita G*) and was thus almost contemporary in its use of minister/*diakonos* with letters written by Paul and his colleagues in the early Christian churches.

> One day Aesop was working in the fields. He was a simple and good man and knew more about the fields and about the animals that lived there and about the life of mortal beings than he was ever able to say. For Aesop had been dumb from birth.
>
> As Aesop was working, a stranger came across the fields to ask him the way. Aesop could not speak but he had good eyes for seeing, and in the stranger he saw the goddess Isis. He bowed in reverence before her.
>
> Aesop could only makes signs to show the stranger the way. But the sun was hot, and in his kindness Aesop offered the stranger his own food and water to help her on her

way. And in the heat of the afternoon he went aside to the shade to rest and sleep.

The stranger did not forget the kindness of the man in the field. She was not really Isis. Isis was the precious bond of the universe, and this fair form was her herald on earth. And now she prayed that Isis would reward Aesop for his kindness.

Isis heard her prayer. While Aesop slept in the fields, Isis sent Aesop the power of speech, and she sent the Muses to give him the gift of noblest eloquence.

Isis did this because Aesop had shown the way to her straying messenger from heaven *(diakonos)*.

Aesop woke up, his tongue was loosed, and he began to give names to what he saw around him, the hare, the lamb, the ants, and the lion.

Winged feet

Hermes, known to many through the Latin mythology as Mercury, son of Zeus and Maia, and, as he boasts, grandson of Atlas, was mischievous and efficient. For him efficiency meant speed because, among his several roles, being messenger of Zeus held priority. As often as not, Zeus' messages were assignations with mortal women and because, as Maia observed, lovers tended to be hasty Hermes had to be smart about his task. But he had other jobs to fit in. He was a cupbearer to the gods, and since most of these had very little to do this could keep him busier than he would have wished. He had also on occasion to convey the dead to Hades, which could involve him, as we shall see, in tête-à-tête with Charon that he could do without. He liked to fit in a bit of thieving, too. One haul as a child, on Lucian's account at least, was Poseidon's trident, Ares' sword, Apollo's bow and arrow, and Hephaestus' smithing tongs. Mortals respected this naughtiness and made him the patron of thieves. One fed-up Athenian who had been robbed of a lambswool cloak left a not very pious prayer wishing the thief to hell and that Hermes the messenger/*diakonos* would take him there. No doubt this was on the principle of setting a thief to catch a thief. He was the patron of merchants, too, but whether this was because merchants were considered shifty and two-timers or because their trading took them on many laborious journeys it might be polite not to enquire.

For all his chattiness Hermes had his serious moments; his presence at a banquet was esteemed as promoting good conversation. In the fifth book of Heliodorus' impossibly romantic novel, *Theagenes and Chariclea* (perhaps familiar to readers also as *The Ethiopians*), on the occasion of a sacrificial feast in honour of Hermes, the rogue merchant Nausicles is well pleased with himself for having traded the fair virgin Charicleia for a precious stone that he was more enamoured of and settles down to relax in conversation over the wine. His companion compliments him on the whole arrangement and cannot fail to see the connection with the god of discourse whom they had just honoured in sacrifice.

> I am filled with admiration at the sumptuousness of your sacrifice, and I cannot think how anyone could render Hermes more propitious than by making a contribution to the feast of the thing which is appropriate to Hermes— discourse.

To the Hellenist Christian, Luke, Hermes was never far out of mind. In one story from the hinterland of Asia Minor, when Paul and Barnabas find themselves among the god-enthusiasts of those parts, they are wildly received as gods visiting earth; the priest of the temple of Zeus organised bullocks for the sacrifice and flowers for the sacred garlands of the banquet, while the mob recited their theology and made Barnabas their Zeus and Paul their Hermes. Luke explains that they did their theology this way because Paul was 'pre-eminent in speech' (Acts 14.12).

These people of Lystra were speaking the native Lycaonian language of the region, but had they spoken Greek Paul and Barnabas would have heard through the hubbub much mention of minister/*diakonos*. Another Hellenist from the century before Luke, Diodorus Siculus, would have understood this scene as clearly as Luke because he too had written in appreciation of Hermes' 'clarity in expounding everthing given into his charge' and had praised his 'art of the precise and clear statement of a message' (5.75.2). A later writer knew that the reason Hermes was 'pre-eminent in speech'—to re-use our translation of Luke's phrase because the Greek here is almost identical—was because he was 'the guardian of true knowledge of the gods' (Iamblichus, *De Mysteriis* 1). Luke was aware of such popular perceptions and of the dangers to his gospel if men like Paul were to be taken for 'gods in the likeness of men' (Acts 14.11), and for this reason, I suspect, was careful never to call any of his heroes of the mission *diakonoi*/ministers, even though he saw great value in calling the mission a *diakonia*. He wanted no confusion in the minds of his Greek readers and listeners about the kind of ministry/*diakonia* they were receiving or about the kind of messenger/*diakonos* who effected it. These were men who were engaged in a ministry to deliver a message about God's deeds on earth; they were not men —much less godlike men—who were visiting this earth with news of their god from heaven.

Heaven was Hermes' home, and he begrudged the time he had to spend rushing down to Hades or about the Aegean sea and beyond on errands for Zeus, at least that is how the irreverent Lucian liked to present him (*Dialogues of the Gods* 24):

> ... here I am only just back from Sidon, where he sent me to see after Europa, and before I am in breath again—off I must go to Argos, in quest of Danae, 'and you can take Boeotia on your way,' says father, 'and see Antiope.' I am half dead with it all.

Lucian, who wrote a century after the first Christians, depicts in one essay an encounter between Hermes and Charon, the boatman of the underworld who conveys souls of the deceased across the river of the dead. On this occasion Charon calls out to a passing Hermes to take him on a tour of the earth where all the souls come from. Hermes has to decline, however, because he is on his way 'to deliver something concerning mortal affairs for the God above'; for 'deliver' here Lucian writes the verb form of *diakonos* (*Contemplantes* 1). In reply Charon digs deep into his mythology to appeal to Hermes as 'co-conductor' of the dead, that is, the one who shares with him the task of bringing the dead to the underworld, and in this he goes back to Hermes' title of honour in Homer, which is *diaktor*, a poetic cousin of the newer word *diakonos*. Sharers in the Greek culture were totally familiar with this linguistic connection. The great medieval dictionary of Byzantium explains that *diaktor* means 'conveyor of the dead' and as an alternative gives *diakonos (Etymologicon Magnum 268)*.

Getting to heaven

In another essay Lucian aims to poke fun at those who believe that the gods have all the answers. So he puts it into the head of someone who has got into a muddle in the schools of philosophy to fit himself out with a set of wings. His plan is simple. He will fly up to heaven and with some first hand advice up there will settle the unanswered questions once and for all. His name is Menippus, and all goes well. We need not bother with what he finds out in heaven but can take note of a few words between himself and the moon as she sees him passing by. The moon, Selene, is accustomed, of course, to seeing messengers passing that way and takes Menippus for another of them. She, too, as it happens, is fed up with philosophers always wondering who or what she was up there in the sky, and wants Zeus to wipe the lot of them off the face of the earth. Her gentle voice coming out of the silence of the skies rather startles Menippus. 'Get me a message to God,' she called, and Menippus understands at once, because again she used the verb for delivering messages related to the word for the messenger /*diakonos* of the gods (*Icaromenippus* 20).

Almost the same phrase occurs in a piece of religious literature which was probably contemporary with the first Christian literature. *The Testament of Abraham* recounts the blessings the patriarch wished to bequeath. As he came nearer to death, Abraham expressed a desire for one last blessing for himself, which was to be granted a vision of everything his God had made. God's commander-in-chief, Michael, visits him to hear what his last wish might be. Overcome with the honour of such a visit, Abraham seizes his opportunity, nonetheless, to use Michael's high services to get his prayer to God. As one translator put this many years ago, Abraham says, 'be the medium of my word ... unto the most High' (G. H. Box, 9.24). The Greek word used by this ancient Jewish writer is again the verb related to the noun messenger/*diakonos* of the gods.

Josephus, the Jewish historian from this era, adopted the same expression when he wanted to retell in the kind of Greek that his non-Jewish readers would appreciate a story in the life of the prophet Jeremiah. Jerusalem was occupied by the Babylonians, and the surviving leaders approached the prophet to know the mind of the Lord on what they should do. In our translation of Jeremiah's Hebrew text we read the reply of the prophet (42.4 *RSV*):

> I have heard you; behold, I will *pray to* the Lord your God according to your request, and whatever the Lord *answers* you I *will tell* you...

Here I have emphasised the words *pray*, *answer*, and *tell*, because these are indicating the process of intercession and communication that is to go on in this circumstance. The prophet is in the middle between the people and God; he will go to God in prayer and bring back a response to the people. There is of course no suggestion that the prophet is to visit God's abode, like Michael or Menippus in the preceding passages, but he is to mediate in a prophetic mode. For Josephus this is simply and effectively expressed in Greek through the *diakon-* verb. His Jeremiah has only to say that he will '*diakon-*/mediate with God on their behalf' for his Greek readers to know that the prophet is about to engage himself in the religious business of getting messages to and from heaven (*Antiquities* 10.177). Coincidentally, in the episode of Josephus' own prophetic role to which we paid close attention at the beginning of this chapter, Josephus cast himself as a *diakonos* and went on, in recounting his role as an intermediary between the Roman commander Titus and the besieged Jews of Jerusalem, to cast himself in the role of Jeremiah.

In translating this passage of Jeremiah we notice that the Greek bible, the Septuagint, which was made for Greek-speaking Jews over two hundred years before Josephus, simply uses an ordinary word for 'pray'. And this was good translation, but the comparison with the smarter translation by Josephus reminds us that the Jews who made the Septuagint seemed in fact to have a dislike for the *diakon-* words, hardly ever using them in their vast work. In all likelihood this was because the words were so suggestive to them and to Jews living in the Hellenistic diaspora of the ways of the Greek gods with humans. Let us move a little closer to that world.

The in-between world

Plato shows us how intimately associated the *diakon-* words were with the Greek way of thinking about the religious connection between this world and the world of the gods. The most immediate lines of communication between gods and mortals, and the public and official lines, were through priests and diviners. Priests were the leaders of sacrifice and were usually identified with the kings in cities which had kings, or with public officials in times of republican rule. Sacrifices were often civic festivals, and the people who gathered at them to feast and sing or perform were conscious that their city was about its business with its gods. Likewise divination or the pronouncing of oracles enjoyed a high civic profile, the city fathers or prominent public officials, as well as the lowliest citizen, sending to a speaker of oracles to know the fate allotted by the gods.

Given that these parts of their religion were so public and so closely tied to priests and to diviners, we can understand why Plato turned his mind to them when he was looking for candidates within society as he knew it who might qualify for the highest role within society as he would like society to be. To know whether a diviner or a priest might be the one who would best head the state Plato analyzed the function of each, and he characterized each function as 'diaconic' (*diakonos*). He says that the diviners practice 'a diaconic skill' because they are interpreters for the gods to humans, and that the priests in their turn practice 'a diaconic skill' because they give gifts to the gods from mortals and by petition win gifts for mortals from the gods (*Politicus* 290c-d).

The Jewish philosopher, Philo, who was a contemporary of the early Christians, shared with Plato this way of talking about priests. Viewing life from God's point of view, he sees God needing a mediator engaged in the process of reconciling humans to himself who will also be 'the mediating agent' who will extend his blessings to men and women. His word here is *-diakonos* (*de specialibus legibus* 1.116). He uses the same word to depict the priests as 'intermediaries bearing God's powers' (1.66). In Philo's world there is a whole intermediate range of activity between the great Creator and the merely finite and visible. Sharing responsibilities there are those souls which have not yet become embodied; they are God's agents (*diakonoi*) in governing mortals (*de Gigantibus* 12).

Other philosophers discussing the merely profane processes in which they perceived mediation to be at work similarly wrote of 'diaconic' function. Alexander of Aphrodisias recognises the 'diaconic' process, for example, in the way colour reaches us through an intervening body of water (*de Mixtione* 5): the water itself is not coloured but transmits the colours of other objects. Similarly, one material, like a piece of glass, can, by transmitting the heat of the sun, cause something else to burst into flame without itself catching fire; by nature it mediates/*diakon-* (*in Aristotelis Meteorologicorum libros* 19). In analysing the functions of our sense faculties Themistius points out one basic difference between touch and other senses; in touch we are in direct contact with what we touch, whereas when we hear a sound we are some distance from the source of the noise and need, he says, an intervening body to carry the sound; he writes of 'a body mediating/*diakon-* in between' (*in de Anima* 125). When Ammonius wants to explain how ideas come to human beings, he ascribes them to the process of communication through language where the human voice 'acts as a medium' between one soul and another; again, *diakon-* (*in Aristotelis Categorias* 15).

All the expressions we have been picking out from ancient literature and philosophy are showing us that the Greeks had a rather subtle tool of language in these *diakon-*words. The words could apply over a good range of activities, and were especially useful when a writer needed to convey an idea to do with mediation. At the same time, we ought to bear in mind that Greeks were not using these words all the time. Many writers never used them at all. But in such instances of their use as we have we easily see that the words had some special usefulness and that they were well suited for talk in matters concerning relations between gods and mortals. In this of course the words could add significant perspectives to the way we view what early Christians were trying to say to us in choosing them for what we call ministry.

One of the most striking passages from this point of view is from the Neoplatonist philosopher, Iamblichus, who began his tract on *The Mysteries* reflecting on the difference between the divine and the creaturely. What marks the divine, he concluded, is the power to rule and determine, to set the course of the universe. Apart from that the divine does not have a role in the created sphere. To ensure that the course of the universe duly unfolds, however, according to divine purposes, the creator has supplied creaturely beings, daemons, superior to mere mortals, who conduct the sphere of things. To humans they may appear divine, but their role is only to do what the gods require; in short, they are 'diaconic' or ministers of the divine (1.20).

Ministers of state

Ministerial activity, in the sense of fulfilling the responsibilities of one's office within governmental, political, and military spheres, is also expressed by the ancient Greeks as *diakonia*, in this way comparing closely with our sense of ministry within government except—and the exception is important—that the Greeks were not using the words in a technical sense. Thus their governments contained officers or used agents who may occasionally be recorded by a writer as having engaged in some ministry/*diakonia* or other, but minister/*diakonos* was not a designation or title of any officer, as *minister* is with us. Demosthenes actually played part of his defence against attacks by Aeschines around the distinction between the designation of office/*arche* and this general term for an undertaking/*diakonia* under a mandate from the state; Aeschines conceded the distinction (Aeschines 3.13-16; Demosthenes 18.311).

To minister/*diakon-* is for Plato also a general term for carrying out duties within the republic (*Laws* 955c). And here and there among other writers we encounter prominent men being thus designated as they go about their public engagements. Dio Cassius refers to a procuratorship of Gaul as a ministry/*diakonia* (54.21.4); Paenius records Vespasian, the future emperor, as the Roman general who held the mandate to bring war to the Jews (6.18.5); and, in defence of the high principles under which the Athenian generals Miltiades and Themistocles carried out war against the Persians, Aristides puts the argument that they were not merely under a mandate from the state but under a mandate of the gods, adding that to minister/*diakon-* for one's superiors is man's noblest and greatest capacity (2.198-199).

The writings of Josephus contain numerous instances of the author designating mandates of different kinds in this way. In the bitter confrontation of the Jewish deputation with Petronius, legate to Syria of the Emperor Gaius (Caligula) who wanted his own statue erected in the Temple enclosure of Jerusalem, Petronius constantly tried to placate the Jews by stating that he was merely carrying out his mandate (*Antiquities* 18.262-304). That argument did not hold for the senior officers in Caligula's body-guard whose consciences could no longer cope with carrying out imperial mandates to torture and to kill (*Antiquities* 19.41,42), and assassinated the emperor. In retelling the fate of Haman in the tale of Esther, Josephus works a neat Greek phrase to report the biblical passage. The bible relates that when the king asked Haman how best to reward a deserving person, Haman outlined a glorious array of honours, thinking he was in line for them himself; the king however replied: 'Make haste, take the robes and the horse, as you have said, and do so to Mordecai the Jew' (Esther 6.10); whereas Josephus writes, 'Be the minister/*diakonos* of what you have advised me so well about' (*Antiquities* 11.255).

At God's table

Among the numerous forms of ministry/*diakonia* we have been encountering in these passages from Greek literature we have not met any slaves. Nor has any form of the ministry/*diakonia* been of a slavish kind, although we recognize that in one instance of killing and torture it was of an unworthy kind. In that instance the ministry remained nonetheless a mandate from the highest worldly authority, namely, the Roman emperor; the origin and authority of the mandate, and the level at which it was to be carried out, were thus of the highest order. Moreover, those performing other kinds of ministry/*diakonia* have also belonged to ranks of society—or of the gods and spiritual beings—with which we do not associate any derogatory connotation. On the contrary, they have belonged to esteemed levels of society. In such ways is the character of a usage built up. From the ways writers use their words, from the associations the words gather from the kind of use they are put to, and from the level of language they are put to work at, we come to know their meaning in particular applications.

In the section of this chapter called *The servant myth* (pages 86-88) we met an assessment of ministry/*diakonia* totally different from the kind we have been forming. The assessment began at the level of waiting at tables. Because waiting at tables was considered to be a slavish action, the *diakon-* words were given a place among the terminology of the ancient Greek servile state and culture. From this level, the scholarly comment informed us, the early Christians selected the words for the purpose of matching their values with the values they perceived in a Son of man who came 'to serve' (*diakon-*, Mark 10.45).

Because our own perception of the Greek ministries is at odds with this contemporary view, a good step for us now will be to test our own view in the same literary environment of waiting at tables which gave rise to the contemporary view. By considering passages which report servants and slaves attending on tables, we should encounter instances of the *diakon-* words which will enable us to characterize the usage in this connection. We need to be reminded, however, that most ancient writers refer only incidentally to this aspect of eating and drinking, and to build up an adequate picture of waiting at table on the basis of these literary fragments would require many minute references and become tediously academic. One way to dodge that effect and yet achieve our purpose will be to work through a few of the passages where an ancient author has spent a little time elaborating his scene. Before sampling that material we will look at one precious source put together by Athenaeus under the Greek title *Deipnosophistae,* a title we might translate as *Philosophers of the Dinner Table.*

Philosophers of the Dinner Table is a long book from around the end of the second century CE. The reference books tend to list its author as a linguist, but Athenaeus would be disappointed to be pigeon-holed like that. In this book he at least tried to work a format with an appeal to the reader. Today we still enjoy eavesdropping at dinner tables by way of published diaries and the gossip of newspaper columnists. We get inklings about the character of individuals we have heard of but are never likely to meet, we hear what they ate and how much they drank, we pick up ideas for menus and for arranging parties. Athenaeus worked up a format on these lines, allowing his philosophers to do the talking, but he was less intent on gossip and personalities than on registering information and opinions across as broad a tract of life as he could swing the table conversation to.

Among the large array of topics in the book are a number which throw up references to servants and slaves. Naturally, the topic of slavery is itself one of these. Another topic is religious festivals, because these required attendants to apportion shares of the sacrificial meat and of the wine to the devotees; related to festivals is the role of the cook, a poor word in English for the man responsible for the ritual slaughter and preparation of the meat; he also required assistants. Dinner parties in grand houses and reports of the eating customs of foreigners or barbarians are likewise occasions for talk about servants. On each of these topics we have not only what the learned gentlemen of this book think but in addition a wide range of views gathered from ancient and contemporary literature on the subject. In fact the philosophers try to outdo each other in the parade of their learning. For today's scholars this aspect of Athenaeus' book is probably its most significant because in its pages are preserved fragments of many works which are otherwise lost to the world. For our purposes, however, the book's advantage is that on the topic of servants and waiting at tables we get both the view of the author himself and then the views in the literary passages his characters refer to.

We are calling the setting of the book a dinner, but the ancient Greek arrangements for a dinner were more complex than ours. The guests—and the occasion was for men only—were not seated around a table but were reclining or sitting on cushions, and low tables were brought to them, each with a course laid out on it. As the courses passed, servants took some tables away and brought in others. This was for the main courses, which together formed the dinner proper or *deipnon*. At its conclusion a second stage of the gathering began, so separate that other guests might be invited for it. This was for the drinking of wine, which was accompanied by tables of desserts, and could be the occasion of musical performances, dancing, and even games. The wine gave its name to this part of the gathering, *symposion*, or 'drinking together'. This was not just an occasion to indulge in wine, but was an occasion to celebrate wine, which was the gift of the gods, to whom, in fact, the first wine of the night was poured out in tribute. It was always mixed with water, the mix being at the discretion of the host. The *symposion* had a ritual air to it and was very ancient. Naturally it required servants, who might be given the formal name of cupbearers.

Such is the setting in which Athenaeus writes of different kinds of servants. If we look at those moments in his *deipnon* and *symposion* when servants bring in new courses or attend to cupbearing duties, we find that Athenaeus uses several words from the group that the ancient Greeks used for servants and slaves (*pais, oiketes*, and others) but never *diakonos*. Nor is this word or its cognates among terms used by his characters in the discussion of the orders of slavery. The only uses of the words by his characters are in the citations from poets and historians which embellish their discourse, and these all bear reference to the rituals of dining; because almost all these are known to us only in these fragmentary citations, we will not attempt to present the detail here.

The *diakon*- words would thus already seem to be used differently from other words for servants. When we look at Athenaeus' own practice, we see why this is so. Not having used the words to designate the ordinary servicing of the guests' at his banquet, Athenaeus turns to them when he is reflecting on the significance of the *symposion* within Greek culture. In this context Athenaeus reveals some of the deeper motivation which set him to compile his book on dining. From at least Homeric times, for the Greeks to gather over food and drink required the presence of their god, to whom the first offering of food and drink was made. The presence of the god enjoined respect on the part of all. The gathering became an acknowledgement of their common Greek heritage, of their historic protection under the gods, and of their commitment to their shared values. Highest among these was their identity as Greeks, to whom the greatest indignity would be subjection to barbarian rule or the loss of individual freedom. With this in mind, we appreciate the force of the following statement by Athenaeus (192b):

> With the Greeks of old the only reason for gathering to drink wine was religion, and any garlands, hymns or songs they used were in keeping with this, and the one who was to do the waiting [*diakon-*] was never a slave; rather young sons of free men would pour the wine ... just as we read in fair Sappho of Hermes pouring wine for the gods.

We notice here the emphasis on freedom, the essence of the Greek ideal, and how the ideal must not be compromised by association with something less worthy through the services of a slave. Other writers witness to customs of waiting at tables which enshrine the same ideal. We shall read one of these shortly. Next, from the beginning of these few lines, we notice how a sense of religion comprehends all, giving meaning to the flowers, the songs, and the formalities attending the drinking of the wine. The mention of Hermes is not coincidental. What is good for the gods is a privilege for mortals to share, and in the rituals of the cupbearing god mortals have the rationale and model for their own *symposion*. From such an idealistic presentation of the meaning of the Greek banquet does the ministry/*diakonia* of attending to tables take its colour and religious value.

A ritual for kings and worshippers

A little over a century ago scholars published an inscription from a remote and mountainous corner of Asia Minor. The inscription had been cut at the command of King Antiochus I of Commagene in the first century BCE. Unlike many other royal inscriptions, this was not a celebration of a military campaign but was a proclamation or, indeed, the revelation that the king was God. In celebration of the divine presence, the inscription lays down the rituals to be observed at the annual sacrifice and banquet commemorating the divine epiphany, which was the king's birth, and the royal coronation. Regulations for the vesting of the priest, rubrics for the presentation of gifts and for the execution of the sacrifice to the king are all a prelude to the culmination of the solemn ritual when the god-king decrees that all, both native and stranger, are to participate in the communal feast. They are to enter the holy precinct and be ministered to *(diakon-)* from vessels which the god has consecrated.

The historian Bato of the second century BCE tells of a ritual in Thessaly which is cast on a more human scale but is of no less religious import. King Pelasgus was confronted one day by a stranger who reported the marvel of a lake giving way to the surfacing of new plains. The king responded to the news as to a message from God and set about honouring the bearer of the message. The stranger was to be the centre of a festive meal. The king's other guests were instructed to join him in attending on the new guest, but the king himself was the only one who carried out the ministry *(diakon-)*. According to Bato, as reported by Athenaeus (640a), the mysterious occasion was the origin of the Thessalonian festival of 'kindly fellowship' when prisoners were freed, and strangers and slaves were received as guests while the masters of households performed the ministry *(diakon-)*.

In such ways does the ministry/*diakonia* of tables appear in Greek literature. As noted above, as basic to its character as religious ritual is the quality it attains through the nobility of the freedom of its ministers. Nothing servile or slavish attaches to providing either the food which has been given to the gods or the wine which has been the gift of the gods to mortals. The Jewish philosopher and apologist, Philo, a contemporary of early Christians, was conscious of the Greek claims for the high religious significance of their *symposion*, and drew a rather forced comparison between it and a religious ritual of the Jewish sect of the Therapeutae, whose name means 'worshippers' and whom Philo is intent on presenting as the only true worshippers. His purpose was to illustrate how their Jewish ritual meal enshrined a much nobler religious ideal than the Greek, which he portrayed as merely sensuous and degrading. As a feature of either ritual he presents ministry/*diakon-*, ensuring only that in the case of the Greeks it is defiled by the presence of slaves while among the Therapeutae, in a truly 'holy *symposion*', only free men perform 'the ministerial duties' (*De vita contemplativa* 70-71).

Special words

In both Philo and Athenaeus we surely detect propagandists of Jewish and Greek rituals. To sort out the rights of either claim is not our business. We are simply observing what ancient writers made of the ritual of ministry/*diakonia*. This designation would seem to be especially marked by them for use of religious ritual. As such, the usage reflects characteristics which we have been observing in other areas: thus, the *diakon-* words provide a title for a god, designations for messages to and from heaven, for operations of the powers under God, and for the processes of prophecy and of intercession. These are all uses within the sphere of religion. As applying to the profane sphere, the words designate undertakings of high moment by persons of some distinction. Were we to provide a full coverage of usage, we would encounter instances of the words applying also to the functions of menial attendants; what we would be drawing attention to in the usage would be the quality of the language and the character of the literature, finding that we were on the highly literate levels of orators, barristers, philosophers, and writers of satire and romance.

Having seen as much as we have, however, we are in a good position to return to some early Christian statements about ministry in the church which have proved critical in the development of contemporary views about ministry. The first of these is the passage we began with from Ephesians.

8: Ministry as Office

Readers who have spent time on other books about ministry in the early church will have noticed that here we have not become involved in trying to identify and differentiate the roles of those who performed various functions within the first Christian communities. Who were *elders* or *presbyters* and what did they do? Or *bishops*—perhaps we should call them *overseers*? And then there were *deacons*. Is the coupling of *overseers and deacons* as we first meet the words in Philippians 1.1 just a composite Greek expression for what the Jewish Christians called *presbyters*? And what about *teachers* and the popular but problematical *prophets*? This exercise has been done again and again in the forty years since Eduard Schweizer's book on *Church Order in the New Testament*, and while it yields a lot of information about what the various titles seem to mean it has clearly not provided enough new insights into what churches basically think they are doing in ministry, otherwise there would not be so much talk about a crisis in ministry nor would the ecumenical impasse in ministry look so redoubtable.

Of course in times prior to our own, one might say from 1950 back to the period of the Reformation, enquiries along these lines were intense and often bitter affairs. A book usually set out to defend a particular style of church organization, often allowing itself generous space to denigrate attempts to defend or promote some other style. Anything to do with bishops, for example, was argued with a huge amount of scholarship and not a little invective because some churches had bishops, indeed considered them to be the authentic sign that a group of believers was a church, while other churches got along quite nicely without them, indeed considered them an aberration. This debate was not just between Protestants and Roman Catholics but was actually more minutely argued among churches coming from the reform like Anglican and Presbyterian. As for the more intransigent debate between Protestants and Roman Catholics, the sticking points here were the role of the bishop of Rome as Pope and the kind of priesthood claimed among the Roman Catholics for their ordained. Our daily language still shows signs of these ecclesiological contests, being littered with words like *priest, pastor, minister, parson, presbytery, manse, vicarage,* and so on, which people who have been brought up in the various denominational traditions use with impeccable propriety.

When early in the present century churches began to come together in ecumenical consultations, decades passed before they introduced the question of their different styles and systems of ministry to the agenda, and then such were the difficulties and tensions that delegates to the consultations counted themselves fortunate to be able to leave agreeing to differ. Conferences at Lausanne (1927), Edinburgh (1937), and Lund (1952) produced nothing on which to build for the future; in fact, at Lund the question was left aside. Great was the satisfaction, accordingly, at the Fourth World Conference on Faith and Order at Montreal in 1963 when a working principle for a shared theology of ministry emerged—not without a tussle—in the proposition that ministry is not the exclusive prerogative of the ordained but is the responsibility of all the baptized.

This principle, as we have had ample occasion to note in chapter 2 above, has transformed approaches to the problem which for centuries ministry had presented any time one church might speak to another of an ecumenical accommodation in the practice and reception of ministry. The general acceptance of the principle has also occasioned this book, which repeats what its academic predecessor attempted to demonstrate, namely, that if under *ministry* we mean to embrace what the early Christians included under their word *diakonia,* the principle is wrong. Not all Christians can be ministers.

Ministers of gospel and mystery

This reminder of where the thinking now stands on churchwide ministry is the appropriate point for us to return to what we called a normative passage in the letter to the Ephesians (4.11-12). What we did with this passage in chapter 2 was to illustrate how in recent decades an almost universal consensus has arisen that in chapter 4 verse 12 we are to understand that the role of the teachers is to equip the baptized for ministry, whereas across preceding centuries the widely—although never universally—agreed position was that ministry was the work whereby the teachers equipped the saints and nurtured them to maturity in knowledge and love. What we will do now is make clear that in view of what ministry/*diakonia* was for Greeks, whether Christian or not, the writer of this letter could not possibly have entertained the idea of all the saints being called into ministry.

In aiming to make this clear, however, we will not be engaging in a set piece of academic exegesis or interpretation. What we propose to do rather is to provide in a non-technical form the results of what close exegesis might come up with. After all we have already worked our way through a large amount of material which has built up our appreciation of what the term ministry/*diakonia* can contribute to a piece of ancient writing about church. We might just remind ourselves, however, that our concentration on this one term has been prompted by the nature of the debate which theologians and ecumenists have been carrying on. As just noted, in the modern discussions about ministry the focus shifted away from the individual offices like that of bishop or elder to what was considered to be the more fruitful area of ministry in general. The reason is simple. The word *diakonia* is where the word *ministry* came into English from (not of course in an etymological sense but, via Latin translation, as an idea). A recent—and I must say succinct and penetrating—essay on 'Ministry in the New Testament' by Roy A. Harrisville has the same narrow focus, while J. T. Forestell's even more recent study, *As Ministers of Christ* (the title itself being one of Paul's minister/*diakonos* phrases) also develops from here. Both writers have much in common with the trend of the present book although, with a fuller appreciation of what Paul's *diakonia* comprised, they could develop further at significant and indeed vital points. For Forestell this would be to the full inclusion of women, and for Harrisville to the link which ministry/*diakonia* necessarily forges between the saving event and the process and tradition of ministry.

In drawing up a profile of ministry as practiced by Paul and recorded by Luke we found its highest feature to be an involvement in and responsibility for the ministry of the word. In Paul especially we found this ministry intimately associated with the process of purveying to believers the mystery of God's saving intention for men and women. Through this ministry, that is, on the occasion of the ministry and through its efficacy, believers actually experience an encounter with the mystery at some level or in some aspect depending on the openness of the minister to the divine word and of the believer to its power of enlightenment. We might refer once more in illustration of this to Paul's exposition of the process of ministry in 2 Corinthians 3.2-18, drawing attention in particular to the outcome of the process so boldly stated in verse 18 that believers, both minister and those who have received God's word through him, 'are being changed into [the Lord's] likeness from one degree of glory to another'.

From a later period—either of Paul's life or of the churches associated with him—we encountered in Colossians 1.13-23 another powerful evocation of this association of ministry with the mystery God has in store for believers. In this passage, being the purveyor of the mystery is what constitutes Paul the minister. What Luke's profile of ministry in Acts adds to this, apart from ministry's absolute authority, is the exclusive prerogative to ministry of those whom the Lord or the church commissions, if indeed this characteristic is not already clearly implied in the altogether special role Paul ascribes to the minister. To suspect this is the case we need only recall the peremptory way Paul dismissed claims to ministry of those whom he considered not to be commissioned to it.

Accordingly, as we move into the exposition on the nature and calling of the church as laid out in the letter to the Ephesians, we are alerted to the fact that ministry is of this same kind when we find the writer engaging with mystery and revelation at the beginning of chapter 3—at least this is where he spells out those words; he has actually been celebrating and expounding the mystery from the beginning of the letter. We notice that at the end of chapter 2 the writer has also tied the experience of the mystery in faith to the teaching of the apostles and prophets of the past, which makes of Paul and contemporary apostles and prophets an extension among the Gentiles of those predecessors (verse 5). Only through his election by God, in a liberal divine gift, which worked powerfully in him, did Paul become a minister/*diakonos* (verse 7). As such a minister, he is to make known 'the plan of the mystery' (verse 9). And as a result of the work of this minister, Christ can dwell by faith in the hearts of men and women (verse 17).

The Ephesian principle

The common experience of life 'in the unity of the Spirit' (4.3) makes of the group of believers 'one body' (verse 4); at the same time believers experience the mystery at different levels or in different degrees (verse 7). Accordingly the writer wishes to put before the believers a vision of what the common experience can lead to. A condition of any organic unity and growth among them, however, is that all realise they are under the grace or gifting of Christ. He is the source of all the life and enlightenment. That comprehended (verses 7-10), the writer moves into outlining both the process by which the unity and growth is achieved (verses 11-14) and the profile of the fully developed body of believers (verses 15-16).

Throughout these phases of growth—always under the Spirit and in the gift of Christ—the controlling principle of life is the enlightenment shared by the believers. Unity of faith and knowledge (verse 13) and freedom from confusion (verse 14) allow the body of believers to mature and fill out to the stature of Christ himself. The enlightenment does not just arrive from on high however, among a number of lucky individuals, nor does it remain and increase within the body of believers by its inherent energy or through the interplay of faith and knowledge among the believers; it is not self-sustaining and does not originate in the gifting of individuals, as if Christ gathered believers to himself by random selection among the Gentiles. On the contrary, according to the writer, Christ ensured that a body of believers would form by giving first a group of suppliers or practitioners of enlightenment. These are the apostles, prophets, evangelists, pastors and teachers (verse 11) whose tasks it is no longer possible for us to determine exactly but whose general responsibility in the provision and maintaining of enlightenment among the body of believers is clear. To the recipients of the letter, on the other hand, the character and the differentiation of roles among these were well known because the writer has simply had to list the functionaries, some of whom, in particular apostles and prophets, may have been remembered from an earlier stage in the development of the churches.

If these functionaries of verse 11 have the general responsibility of sustaining the church in unity of faith, we have only to follow the writer one step further to know how they are to carry out their responsibility. This step takes us into verse 12, whose fate under the judgement of modern translators we have observed in chapter 2. Here we will review the verse from the first edition of the *Revised Standard Version*, reading that Christ has given as gifts these sets of teachers 'for the equipment of the saints, for the work of ministry/*diakonia*, for building up the body of Christ...' Again we come to our question, whose ministry is this? This time our answer is confident and well founded. Without needing to look for meaning through subtle considerations of the grammatical structure and interrelationship of the phrases here, we can be certain that the ministry/*diakonia* belongs to the teachers. The context requires it, and the Greek word itself demands it. Let us remind ourselves why.

The writer has prepared us for a consideration of this ministerial arrangement for the church through his reflections on the role of the minister/*diakonos* within the purveying of mystery (3.7). This was just a few hundred words earlier, and the general context has not changed; rather the context has grown richer with the marvels of heaven's mystery as it has narrowed to a vision of the church as the precinct of heaven's gifts. Further, conscious of the weight and character of both the term minister/*diakonos* and the term ministry/*diakonia* in any context of revelation or of message from heaven—we can think back to how effective these words were in the stories presented in chapter 7 about Josephus as a prophet, about Aesop recognizing the messenger of Isis, about Hermes, and in passages about the sphere in between heaven and earth, as well of course as in the powerful antecedents in the Christian prose of Paul himself in especially 2 Corinthians 3.3-18—we recognize what the author is signalling, namely, that through the process of ministry/*diakonia* the enlightenment by which the church lives is transferred from Christ in the heavenly sphere to the body of believers in the earthly. The transference is what 'the work' (verse 12) is. The transference is that process called *ministry* which we have seen illustrated in the work of one *minister*, Paul, and only a person who is a *minister* can engage in it. A *minister* is one appointed to a task, and in this instance the task is that of providing the believers with the teaching which sustains them in faith and knowledge.

Perhaps enough has been said to establish that to appreciate the import of this statement in Ephesians 4.11-12 we must recognize the significance of the words in the passage before we begin to juggle the sentence around to find its intent. The writer has contributed the key word ministry/*diakonia* to the sentence for the precise purpose of emphasizing the sacred and exclusive character of the teachers' responsibility. No ancient reader of his Greek phrase could mistake his meaning. When we late twentieth century Christians turn his word into a nondescript service within the capacity of any believer we gravely distort his meaning.

The ministry of the early church, then, on the view of the author of this letter—and one theory has proposed that the author is the slave Onesimus whose father in God Paul became (Philemon 10) and who, as bishop of Ephesus, used this letter to preface the publication of a collection of Paul's own letters—was the work and responsibility of a select number of preachers and teachers. Such work supposed a profoundly religious engagement with the Christian mystery, and was named *ministry* by virtue of this engagement. Implied in the writer's insistence on the need for unity of faith and knowledge is the coherence of the ministry across various functions which the various titles point to as well as the continuity of the ministry from one generation to another. This in turn requires the integration of all the works of ministry through a process or within a framework of synod or of hierarchy. The contribution of the believers to such a process or system is likely to be substantial but it is not critical and it is certainly not constitutive of the ministry. The ministry is constituted by the mandate of the heavenly Christ, maintained and passed on by the holders to others whom they bring under the mandate. What believers might contribute here we leave to the imagination, to hope, to the shared experience of faith, and to freedom under grace. Perhaps we can see believers advocating the causes of those among themselves whom they recognize as worthy candidates for being called into ministry, but the call itself will come finally from the ministers.

Perhaps only one other comment on the Ephesian principle of ministry is necessary. Today's majority are likely to find an exclusive or hierarchical style of ministry repugnant. It flies against the democratic instinct of the age, it runs counter to the strongly charismatic quality attributed to ministry in current thinking, and it seems only to endorse the style of the incumbents of the traditional Christian hierarchies. What we need to recognize, however, is that the hierarchies which many of today's Christians find repugnant are not so much structured on the model of the Ephesian hierarchy as borrowing from the model of political hegemonies of the ancient world. They early became hegemonies for the exercise of political and coercive power within the realm of the people's new religious experiences of Christian faith, and in later times misguidedly appropriated for this jurisdiction within the religious sphere the religious designation 'sacred rule' or hierarchy. The author of Ephesians, however, is speaking of another sphere altogether, unconnected with worldly power and rule, but imbued with authority of an exclusively religious kind nonetheless. The sphere is that of powerless faith and knowledge. Within this sphere everything is enlightening and heartening but nothing can be effected by power, politics, or law. Within it everyone receives from the same source (verse 13) and there are no grades of station. All grow into love (verse 16). That some have the requirement put upon them to ensure the vigor and continuity of faith and knowledge gives them no power but lays them directly under the mandate of Christ. As Calvin put it (*Commentaries*, p. 122), theirs is 'the ministry by which God reigns among us.'

A loss of principle

Calvin wrote that phrase in the introduction to his commentary on the Ephesians. In his treatment of chapter 4,11-14 he emphasizes again and again the official and exclusive character of this ministry; by 'the will of God and the appointment of Christ' the church possesses an 'order' in what he calls 'the external ministry of the Word', namely, the group of men—and for him they could only be men—who are the pastors and teachers (pages 177-184). While insistent, he does seem a little taken aback that God should arrange the church so when by divine power men and women could have been brought directly into salvation 'without human assistance'. Here, of course, he is conscious of the claims of those in his day whom he calls 'the fanatics, who invent secret revelations of the Spirit for themselves' and then of 'the proud, who think that for them the private reading of the Scriptures is enough'. They are a demonstration to him of the waywardness of the human spirit and of how right it is for the church that Christ should 'prescribe the way in which it shall be built', namely, through the 'offices' of 'the outward preaching'.

I return to Calvin not for his authority, which is by no means obvious in all aspects of his reading of these passages, but because writing out of a time which was given over to controversy about the functioning of church he was so overpoweringly convinced of the intent of the author of Ephesians at this point of ministry. Ministry here was an office, and ministers were to be appointed to it, 'colleagues and comrades of one another' over against the rest of the believers: 'such is the Will of God.' As we have said above, this understanding fits exactly the understanding a contemporary Greek would have taken from the author's use of ministry/*diakonia* here. (D. M. Lloyd, a preacher of recent times and expositor of the scriptures, has written with similar vigor in the conviction that the idea 'in the entire context is that of the ministerial offices in the Church', concluding, ' "The perfecting of the saints" cannot happen apart from the work of the ministry' [*Christian Unity: An Exposition of Ephesians 4:1 to 16*, p. 200].)

In our day, by contrast, as we have seen in chapters 1-2, the ministerial order constructed by the author of Ephesians has been dismantled, and all the believers, by virtue of their baptism into Christ from which they all share in his priesthood, are now said, under a significant degree of influence from the distorted reading of this passage, to share in his ministry. We will not go back over how awkward this has made all talk and thought of the ordained ministries in the churches today, but a reminder of the scale of the change is useful. It was precisely the possibility of such a change, for example, that Calvin was anticipating and resisting in his pages here. He knew, and could observe, that with the dismantling of the ecclesiastical offices of the Roman church the body of believers was exposed to any number of enthusiasms which might claim to be the inspiration of the Spirit of God. While, however, within the reformed tradition which he established the enthusiasm was contained by the clarity and efficiency of official ministerial structures, the same effect was not so securely achieved in all reformed churches. In particular, within the Lutheran tradition of ministry, the question of ministry was never satisfactorily resolved. A tension has remained from the beginning, and has expressed itself within different churches at different periods and continues to do so today, as to whether ministry is an office as such or whether it is a function confided to some in the church for the purposes of good order. If it is the latter, all in the church can conceivably possess a ministerial capacity, although only a few are called upon to use it. Of itself—and apart from the fact that the scheme is not compatible with how the early Christians thought of ministry—one might think the scheme could work. In fact, however, it leaves the function of ministry open to a powerful influence. This is the enthusiasm to which Calvin disparagingly referred.

Being enthused, whether as enjoying a spiritual conviction or as being on a spiritual high, is one of the perennial attractions, rewards and dangers of religious experience. In all periods of their history Christians have been enthused in either way. Much good has come of their experiences, as with John Wesley, and much brutality, as in the callous execution of John Huss, and huge tragedies, as in the mass suicides of Jim Jones' disciples. And in theology, in regard to ministry, there is strong undergirding of enthusiasm in the talk of gifts of the Spirit or, in its Greek form, charismata or charisms. Conceived of as a capacity with which the baptized person is endowed, ministry could claim to be called forth in an individual's response to the Spirit. Ministry would thus be in origin and essentially charismatic. One would say, as many do say, that if the church chooses to speak of office, the office must be understood as coming through the gift of ministry. On the contrary, says the author of the Ephesians, ministry is by definition an office, and those called to it are the gift of Christ to the church. The fact that they possess gifts apt for ministry does not make them ministers; they become ministers when they are installed in the office of ministry.

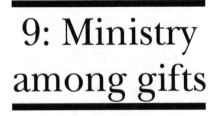

9: Ministry among gifts

Paul is often presented as the champion of a charismatic ministry, and a great amount of exegesis, theology and history has been written to support this cause. The cause is misconceived, however, and its underlying proposition is seriously misleading. In chapter 12 of 1 Corinthians, from where the discussion mainly takes its rise, Paul is proposing that the teaching roles are the roles from which the church takes its cohesion. Through his image of the church as a body he is acknowledging the variety of capacities within a church and endorsing their exercise. In doing so, he is making the point that each capacity is proportionate to the needs of the body and is to be exercised within that scope. No one function is to encroach upon or to impede other functions. And the first functionaries within the body of believers, appointed by God, are apostles, the second are prophets, and the third are teachers (verse 28).

Keeping enthusiasm in check

Within the context of the diversity of the body's functions Paul could hardly have brought greater emphasis to bear than he has here on the priority in the church of the teaching functions. These are the functions which guide, direct, inspire, curtail, develop, train. The body will perform only as well as it is educated. Its many other gifts—its powers of healing, tongues, administration, and so on—show that it is alive and well, but it remains a body, that is, an organic union of many people, by virtue of having been fashioned through the work of the founding preachers, and then nourished by prophets and teachers. As we know from Paul's mind in this letter, this founding work was a collaboration with God (3.9), and in that connection we cannot escape the implication of Paul's conceptualization of himself and of the other collaborators as ministers (3.5). Theirs is the responsibility and prerogative of making the believers into a church. In chapter 3 one image of this work is farmers preparing a crop, another is builders raising a temple; in chapter 12 the image is of a living body, the leading function of which is its consciousness activated at different stages by apostles, prophets, and teachers. Of interest to us over following sections will be to see the relationship between the first two of these. (Of teachers Paul says no more.)

An apostle and a teacher we assume to be such by appointment, but a prophet? A prophet arises, and prophets were a main source of enlightenment and growth for the early communities (Romans 12.6; Ephesians 4.11), and they carry authority because they are placed by God (1 Corinthians 12.28). In the Corinthian church the activity of prophets is more clearly exposed to us than elsewhere, especially in chapter 14. Prophecy is the gift to be desired (verse 1) because prophecy builds up the community, encourages, and consoles (3), and is thus superior to the esoteric experience of speaking in tongues (5); prophecy is intelligent and penetrating, and can reveal the presence of God even to the unbeliever (24-25); accordingly it is to be cherished and dwelt on, and all are free to seek some expression of it, subject always to good order and growth (29-32; 37-40). Thus the utterances of the prophet do not share the exuberant or mysterious quality of what is uttered in tongues (23), but are a measured reflection, subject to the measured critique of companions in the gathering, on the mystery which the believers have gathered to share.

These utterances are a teaching device, deeply affirmative of the shared faith, and they seek also to be illuminating. From what is shared at this level the community gathers greater cohesion and direction. Clearly, from Paul's indications in chapter 14 and from our own perceptions of such a process, not all in a mixed community are equipped for prophecy; some are inhibited by inadequate instruction, others by lack of experience or by spiritual immaturity. The community itself, when it honoured good order, knew its prophets, and nothing in 1 Corinthians 12.1-7 implies that a prophet's role is any less orderly or is to be any more enthusiastic than that of apostle or teacher. Like apostle and teacher, the prophet is bound by the harmonies of the body.

The prophet's authenticity is known in part from the effectiveness with which he preserves and promotes the harmonious growth of the body.

In 1 Corinthians 12.1-11 Paul places these upbuilding functions of prophecy among a number of others as gifts of the Spirit. In doing this Paul is not drawing up a constitution for a church, implying, that is, that a church functions only when it has all the gifts he lists operating effectively. He is being much more realistic than that. He is cutting his coat to suit his cloth. The Corinthian church operates through prophecy and other gifts, they are making enquiries of him about relative values or priorities, and Paul casts his response in their terms and in the light of what he knows of that community. With another community the emphasis would be different. What matters for Paul is that the community draws life from its experience of faith, maintains its unity, and sustains growth.

Splitting up gifts

Because the Corinthians are finding their most intractable problem in the use and disposition of their newfound spiritual skills at worship—how newfound may perhaps be open to question, because some scholars suggest that one of their problems may have been that in their Christian worship they were introducing too much of the ecstatic style of their pre-Christian cults—Paul addresses himself with great deliberation to things of the spirit, beginning here at chapter 12 and concluding only at the end of chapter 14. And his opening observations, for all the warning signals they contain, are very affirming of the convictions which the Corinthians held about the place of the Spirit in their lives, for in 12.1-3 he assures them that everything done in faith and in worship is done by the power of the Spirit. With remarkable rhetorical emphasis he develops and reinforces this teaching down to verse 7, and then illustrates it in a rich medley of spiritual activities down to verse 10, concluding in verse 11 with the same Spirit he had begun with.

Unfortunately and unavoidably our English translations cannot represent the rhetoric with its balances and wordplays. Thus

Paul begins in verses 4-6 with the idea of a wide distribution of heavenly gifts; once distributed across the church, these gifts appear as different kinds of spiritual activities so that the end result is a variety of gifts in the church, and this result is what the translations generally concentrate on in speaking of *varieties* or *different kinds*. In concentrating on the result, however, such translations miss the process which the writer evidently had in mind because his Greek word suggests the act of dividing or splitting something up. Firstly, he uses the word as a noun in verses 4-6 (*diaireseis*), giving it first place (apart from simple conjunctions) in each of the three sentences, thus greatly emphasising it, and then, secondly, after he has illustrated the kinds of gifts he wants to talk about, he returns to his idea in verse 11, this time expressing it by the cognate verb (*diairoun*). Here some of the translations, especially the traditional ones, pick up his idea by printing *dividing*, beginning with Tyndale 1535 and so mostly until the *Revised Version* 1881; the *Revised Standard Version*, too, writes in a similar vein that the Spirit 'apportions to each one'. Thus, the idea of dividing which emerges clearly in the English verse 11 is actually only echoing and re-emphasing the idea already expressed and emphasised in the Greek verses 4-6. This invites us, surely, to look closely at what Paul had in mind with the division of gifts there.

What is being divided up and distributed are *charismata* (translated *gifts*, but the Greek word is often now used in English), ministries/*diakoniai* and *operations*. For this last I use Tyndale's good word, which went through all English translations until the *Revised Version* switched slightly to the sharper *workings*; the Greek is *energemata*, and while the *Revised Standard Version* writes 'varieties of working, but it is the same God who inspires [*energoun*] them all', I prefer to reflect the interplay of the two Greek *energ-* words by writing '*activities* but the same God *activates* them'. Each of these three divisions or distributions is aligned with a distinct divine principle, namely, Spirit, Lord, and God, so that we have the following pattern:

$$
\begin{array}{rcl}
\text{gifts} & - & \text{Spirit} \\
\text{ministries}/\textit{diakoniai} & - & \text{Lord} \\
\text{activities} & - & \text{God}
\end{array}
$$

What to us is reminiscent of a trinitarian formula here is not to distract us from the writer's overriding thought, which is to do with the divine origin of all the powers at work in the church. That is to say, Paul is not specifying the origin of the gifts, the ministries, and the activities in three distinct sources; after all, in one place he writes that 'God activates them all' (verse 6) and in another that 'the Spirit activates them all' (verse 11).

This perhaps leads us to ask what Paul was actually intending to convey through the three-fold division. The three-fold division, especially with the repetition of the leading word *diaireseis/divisions/varieties*, remains a notable rhetorical device, and we might wonder whether Paul has constructed it with only the very simple intent of saying that what is distributed from heaven can be called by different names, or whether he is intending something totally different, namely, that what is distributed from heaven is to be divided up in a number of ways. If his three words are simply a matter of three names for one and the same reality, then we can draw up the following formula:

gifts = ministries = activities

And this would be by far the commonest understanding of the relationship between the three words among those who have written on this section in modern times. Assisting this view is the nearly common understanding of the middle term 'ministries/*diakoniai*' as a term meaning *services to the community*, and commentators are further encouraged in this view by the fact that on Paul's own following statement the heavenly distribution is for the good of the whole community (verse 7: 'to proffit the congregacion', as Tyndale boldly translated); anything anyone does has to be for the better functioning of the body (verse 25) and for the upbuilding of the church (14.12: 'the edifyinge of the congregacion', Tyndale). If we are to read verses 4-6 like this, with the three words as just a string of names each of which applies equally appropriately to activities in the community, we are left with a simple but inspiring passage about God's liberality towards the church. In that case, however, Paul's strong rhetoric would seem to be overplayed, and, what is more telling, we would be reading the passage without taking into consideration what it was possible and what it was not possible for Paul to intend by his term ministries/*diakoniai*.

Paul's interest in ministry/*diakonia* as terminology for saying something specific about roles in the church is basic. In 1 Thessalonians 3.2, if we keep to the reading favoured above in chapter 6, Paul has already in his pastoral career used minister/*diakonos* to lend authority to Timothy's mission among the Thessalonians. With the Corinthians he has already used the same term in chapter 3 verse 5 of this letter to claim the same authority for himself and Apollos and thus cut off at the source a threatening challenge to the unity of the community. And in some of his next writings to the Corinthians he will return to this terminology to stake his strongest claims among them (see 2 Corinthians 11.23 and chapter 4 above). Outside of evangelizing roles, he applies the terminology equally effectively to delegations of Christians to other churches, as in his collection for Jerusalem (e.g. Romans 15.26), in the case of Phoebe (Romans 16.1), and in the case of Stephanas (1 Corinthians 16.15). That is just about the ambit of his uses, and they are not uses peculiar to him but exemplify usage of other Christian and, particularly, other non-Christian Hellenistic and earlier Greek writers.

To look again at the possibilities in our passage, we would have to say that neither Paul nor any other ancient writer could have used the term ministries/*diakoniai* to mean what an eminent earlier German commentator called here 'strictly service to the brethren' (Johannes Weiss, 1910); here, with the mention of the 'Lord', the term can only mean services or *ministries at the Lord's command*. The Lord's command, in other words, is what constitutes them as *ministries*. Our next question, accordingly, is to ask who in this case is thought of as being under the Lord's command. And to consider that we need to return to the structure of Paul's paragraph.

1 Corinthians 12:4-6

In verses 4-6, as we have already emphasised, we are to think of Paul writing about the dividing up of heaven's gifts in the process of distribution. In being divided up, different parts of heaven's gift necessarily go to different individuals; this phase of the process is exemplified very clearly in the way Paul writes verses 7-11, and is the foundation of the image of the body with members functioning in many different ways. Now, how is this concept of the division of heaven's gifts reflected in the sentence structure? In Paul's arrangement of the Greek there may be subtleties which are not easily translated, but if we put a word for word rendering in one central column, and on the left side of it put the *Revised Standard Version* as a point of reference and then, in the right hand column, put a new translation, we may be able to illustrate more effectively and economically than could be explained the subtleties we are confronted with.

RSV	*Word for word*	*New translation*
Now there are varieties of gifts but the same Spirit;	divisions however of gifts exist, but the same Spirit	Divisions exist among gifts, although the Spirit is one and the same:
and there are varieties of service, but the same Lord;	*and* divisions of ministries/*diakoniai* exist, and the same Lord	*both* divisions of ministries [*diakoniai*], the Lord too remaining the same,
and there are varieties of working, but it is the same God who inspires them all in every one.	*and* divisions of activities exist, but the same God the one activating all things in all	*and* then divisions of activities, with God of course remaining the same, the one who activates all these things among all of us.

The main differences introduced in the new translation are three: (1) the word *divisions* instead of *varieties*, and the reason for this change has been discussed; (2) the word *ministries* instead of *service* also for reasons already largely provided and because the word *service* is inadequate and possibly misleading; and then (3) the use of *both/and* instead of *and/and*. The second and third points are connected, and we will look into them together.

Probably the least appreciated aspect of Paul's rhetoric in this passage is his reference to ministries/*diakoniai*. The meaning of *services to the community* has already been rejected. Should we be equally confident that 'the word here has nothing to do with "ministry" in the technical sense', as influential commentators insist? (so C. K. Barrett on p. 284 of his commentary, and see H. Conzelmann, *1 Corinthians*, p. 208) On the contrary, as indicated by a brief review above of how Paul uses this word and in the light of our earlier chapters about general usage, we have no reason to think that Paul would be using the word in any other sense than what the writer has here called a technical sense of ministry. By this we mean a ministry which consists in carrying out the mandate to reveal God's hidden purposes in Christ, namely, the ministry carried out by Paul and others like Apollos. In fact we can say that no other meaning than this is available for this context. His ancient readers—they were actually hearers—were not going to be mistaken in this. This word said to them at once *sacred missions*, and they were totally aware of what these had been among them: had not Paul in the early chapters of this letter pointed to the different *ministers* they had received? (1.10-12; 3.3-6)

Charismata and pneumatika

If this was the import of the word for the Corinthians, we have some adjustment to do in the way we think of the verses 4-6, because the introduction of *ministry* in the sense of *sacred mission* immediately wrecks the three-way equation we set out above: *gifts = ministries = activities*. This equation can no longer stand because the *activities* are activated in everybody (verses 6 and 11) whereas the *ministries* are reserved for the few whom the Lord has committed them to. Thus, instead of the church being presented here as replete churchwide with gifts, ministries, and activities, it is being presented as a church replete with gifts, indeed, but the gifts are of two main kinds, ministries and activities. We can put that in the following diagram:

$$\text{gifts}/\textit{charismata} \left\{ \begin{array}{l} \text{ministries}/\textit{diakoniai} \\ \\ \text{activities}/\textit{energemata} \end{array} \right.$$

Several perspectives of church open up once this diagram is applied (and the division of gifts it represents, if not quite our understanding of them, has also been advocated in recent years by E. Earle Ellis in *Pauline Theology: Ministry and Society*, pp. 35-36). To see these perspectives we need to remind ourselves that the word *charismata* is to be understood just as we have it here as *gifts*, and that meaning is not to be obscured or elaborated by the addition of what we have come to include in the modern English word *charisma*, as applied for example to a politician whose character or public image has an almost irresistible appeal in the electorate, nor with what we associate with the word *charismatic* as applied to gatherings of Christians who give voluble expression to their joy and confidence in the Lord in song and praise, perhaps also in tongues and healings. To associate gifts/*charismata* in such ways with the contemporary sense of *charismatic* is to confuse Paul's idea of *charismata* with Paul's other important word here *pneumatika*/spiritual. Indeed, one may say that the so-called charismatic churches and charismatic movements within churches of today have made it difficult for us to think of *charismata* not being the same as *pneumatika*/spiritual. But it is important, if we are to appreciate how Paul envisages church in this passage, that we distinguish two realities here.

Paul has begun this long section of his letter (chapters 12-14) announcing abruptly, 'Now concerning spiritual *things*'—and our discussion is not helped by the fact that translations from as far back as the Great Bible of 1539 very often insert the word *gifts* here in place of *things*: the Greek has neither of these nouns, being able to use the adjective *pneumatika*/*spiritual* by itself. In verse 1 Paul is not announcing a discussion about *gifts* at all but a discussion about the types of religious experiences which the Corinthians have found exciting and have asked Paul about and which Paul gives us a fairly clear impression of in what he has to say in 12.8-10 and throughout chapter 14. These are *spiritual* or *pneumatic* experiences and activities, and that is what he calls them again as he introduces chapter 14 (the adjective alone *pneumatika* and without the addition of the word *gifts*, which in English goes back for this verse to Tyndale 1535).

In handling this subject for the Corinthians Paul set himself a very clear objective, as we can see from the overall effect of the chapters. Presented with a community giving preference in some of its gatherings to a spiritual or pneumatic experience called speaking in tongues, Paul, who spoke in tongues himself (14.18) and does not want to discourage the practice among the Corinthians (verses 5 and 39), develops a firm instruction on how to moderate the potentially disruptive effect on the gathering of this pneumatic phenomenon and directs them to develop their skills in and give preference instead to another pneumatic activity called prophecy. As he says (verse 19), he would rather teach something in five intelligible words than utter ten thousand words of praise that no one understood.

The moderation of tongues and the nurture of prophecy being his objective, Paul pays little attention to other pneumatic activities apart from acknowledging their presence and value in the community (12.8-10; 14.28-30). (In our discussion here we have no occasion to comment on Paul's treatment of the pre-eminence of love in this context, chapter 13.) What he does give close attention to in the introduction to chapter 12, however, is the place of these spiritual things/*pneumatika* in the way a church is constituted. Only in this context does he speak of them as gifts/*charismata*, but he makes it clear that gifts/*charismata* include more than *pneumatika*. As we have seen in the last diagram, gifts include both *ministries*, which are not *pneumatika*, and *activities*, which are. In other words, everything that a church does faithfully or is capable of doing in faith is charismatic in the sense of being the implementation of heavenly gifts. The Pauline church we see at Corinth is at the same time, within itself, spiritual or pneumatic because it lives and develops from the exercise of the pneumatic activities Paul alludes to. But the sum of its pneumatic energies does not constitute the whole of what God gives to the church because over it and moderating it is the work of the ministry, represented in this case so clearly by Paul. In this case also, it happens that Paul the minister is absent from his charge because his role is to exercise ministry in other churches as well.

Ministry and prophecy

The perspective of church which this understanding of 12.4-6 provides is thus of a group of believers who have been brought together in Christ through the minister's proclamation of the word, who then reflect on this word in the power of the Spirit's illumination and build one another up through the prophetic teaching which emerges from this experience—no less than five times in chapter 14 does Paul urge the community's responsibility for upbuilding—and who remain within the tutelage and guidance of the ministry. Interestingly ministry holds the same place in the perspective of church held by the writer of the letter to the Ephesians (4.12), as we have seen. There too it is a gift of Christ, just as in 1 Corinthians 12.5 it is associated with the name of the Lord. One difference is apparent in that the later writer's larger historical perspective allows him to look back on the whole known development of the churches and to see all those who have relayed the revealed mystery as workers in ministry, whether they be the apostles or prophets of old or the teachers of his own day. The perspective Paul is asking the Corinthians to keep in view is different. He too puts apostles, prophets, and teachers in the first rank of God's appointment for the church (12.28); in this, however, his purpose is not to identify what is the ministerial part of the church, which he had no need to do because the Corinthians knew and had already been reminded in chapters 1 and 3 of who the ministers were, but to make a statement about what functions in the church are more important to it. This issued in a statement that the intelligent encounter with the Spirit in prophecy was of more value in building up a house of the Spirit in Corinth than unintelligible personal encounters which could not be shared with others. Accordingly, Paul concludes, teaching—with the intelligent critique of teaching (14.29

and 32)—is where the communal upbuilding will begin, and this function in the community belongs to 'first apostles, second prophets, third teachers'. In Paul's language, and the Corinthians understood this instinctively also, the only ministry/*diakonia* in this list was that of the apostles, although a later writer was also correct from the point of view of usage to include within his concept of ministry/*diakonia* a wider range of teaching functions.

In everything Paul taught about church in these chapters he was governed principally by the needs of the Corinthian church. In other words, he was teaching what the church in Corinth was or should be, not what *every* church was or could be. Because the Corinthians were becoming confused amid the richness and vitality of experiences which they identified as the work of the Spirit, Paul's objective was to bring them back to somewhere nearer the gospel he had preached to them and to the means whereby knowledge of that would become sounder among them and express itself more surely in their lives and relationships. In the proper understanding of God's ways with the church, made clear in the measured reflections of the prophets among them, their best spiritual experiences would take their rise. The whole church would then be healthily spiritual or pneumatic. Thus in these instructions, as we have said earlier, Paul was not putting together a systematic statement on church, nor in this picture of the spiritual wonders at play in Corinth do we have a prescription for other churches.

From Paul's correspondence with some other churches and from other later writings we get glimpses of how the several congregations ordered their experiences. These are the details that Eduard Schweizer brought to our attention in the book noted at the beginning of chapter 8 (see page 109); because we are not descending to such detail, however, but are concentrating on the notion and place of ministry in the early churches, in this matter we will just point to what still today is the most instructive complement to Schweizer in the way that it isolates the unity and purpose of ministry amidst the diversity of the earliest congregations. This is André Lemaire's *Ministry in the Church*, which is a translation of his French book of 1974, itself developed from his earlier scholarly *Les ministères aux origines de l'église* of 1971). Moving on from there and from how Paul presented the priority and authority of ministry to the Corinthians, we turn to see him on one other occasion acknowledging the complementarity of ministry and prophecy in his words about gifts to the church in Rome.

Paul's thinking in Romans is what he put together in the course of his work and experience among the Corinthians. Not surprisingly some ideas which came to expression in his correspondence with the Corinthians find a developed treatment in the letter to the Romans, while some of the themes elaborated for the Corinthians are expressed more succinctly to the Romans. We see the latter exemplified in the question of gifts (Romans 12.3-8). Here we meet again the concept of the congregation as one body, of the members having different roles, of individuals receiving gifts/*charismata*, of the gifts being different from one person to another according to the measure of faith, plus a list of the leading and some auxiliary gifts. These are, in order, prophecy, ministry/*diakonia*, teaching, exhortation, and other gifts relating to liberality. What we are drawing attention to is the conjunction once again, at the head of the list, of prophecy, ministry, and teaching. Clearly for Paul these are the gifts a church needs—if one prefers, the gifts which God first provides so that a church may be. The interesting factor in this situation between Paul and the Roman church, however, is that Paul has not yet been to Rome: earlier we saw how this circumstance affected Paul's introduction to Rome of Phoebe of Cenchreae (Romans 16.1).

We draw attention to the circumstance because in it is probably the explanation of the odd ordering of the leading gifts, with first prophecy and only secondly ministry. The ministry/*diakonia* (verse 7) certainly includes the ministry of Paul, the one whose reputation as a minister to the farflung churches of the east has preceded his letter to Rome. In placing it second to prophecy Paul is acknowledging that the Roman church owes nothing of its formation to his ministry—and yet he is acknowledging his ministry nonetheless as a prime agent of God's saving power among the Gentiles, as he proclaimed a few pages earlier (11.13) —but in the first place he is acknowledging that the Roman church has grown to its maturity through the workings of prophecy in its midst. No mention here of possible obscuring of the prophetic message through an exuberance of pneumatic energy. Paul simply places the normal processes of church growth as he knew it within the framework of gifts/*charismata* that he had elaborated in his instructions to the Corinthians. Of the status he expected the Roman church to accord to his own ministry/*diakonia* we have no need to enquire; the letter itself speaks for that.

Similarly, in the three chapters of 1 Corinthians 12-14, where Paul leaves interesting historical traces of a search by some of the earliest Christians for their Christian identity—a search too for the appropriate social and ritual expressions of their identity—we have as well a demonstration of the power and authority of Paul's ministry, a ministry which he acknowledges in 12.5 to be as much a gift of God as the minutest revelation of a Corinthian prophet. We would also seem to have an exhibition of one of the constitutive principles of church, namely, that although ministry is a gift and, by the implication of language, also itself charismatic, it is by nature an office among whose responsibilities is the good ordering of other gifts in the church, these being the spiritual or pneumatic gifts. Whereas the Corinthians had led themselves to think that the church was essentially pneumatic—as being, on their understanding of that term, a group of individuals exposed to variegated divine inspirations—Paul was advising them that the church was essentially charismatic or a field of divine giftedness, and that within this field ministries took precedence over the spiritual experiences and activities which they called the *pneumatika*. Accordingly, to the extent that we neglect to take account of the authority inherent in the concept of ministry/*diakonia,* contributions to the debate concerning the relative authority of gift and office—which is a debate initiated a hundred years ago by Rudolf Sohm—are made under a grave handicap. One might even suspect that the debate should never have begun.

Ministry and authority

Paul was to hear worse news out of Corinth than confusion about how Christians should run their gatherings, because other visiting missionaries were soon to be questioning the way he conducted his ministry and even his right to be a minister in the first place. We saw what response this elicited from Paul and what profound insights into ministry his response revealed (chapter 4). At the end of his first letter to the Corinthians, however, problems with ministry are not what he was anticipating. He had been receiving the delegation from Corinth composed of Stephanas and his colleagues, undoubtedly discussing with them the nature and extent of the problems he had given advice on in chapters 12-14 of his letter, and in sending the letter to the church with these returning delegates he recommended them as leaders, as we saw in the story of Stephanas in chapter 6 above. Whether the Corinthians took that advice, we have no way of knowing. If they did, the leaders were in for a rough passage as the community split once again with the arrival of the new missionaries.

From these subsequent developments in the ministry of Paul to Corinth perhaps all we can take to add to our evaluation of early Christian ministry is a perception of how far its authority stretches. And really that is not far at all. If Paul succeeded in having good order established in the meetings of the Corinthian Christians, we would say the authority of his ministry had been vindicated; if the Corinthians acknowledged the authority which Paul had delegated to Stephanas and his colleagues, again Paul's ministry showed its authority. But Paul had no control over the reception of his ministry or over the measure of authority which the Corinthians might attach to it. And in fact he knew that the authority carried by ministry was not a coercive, political, or legal authority but an authority arising from the power of the gospel which ministry made available to believers. The ministry had a capacity to effect change in the lives of individuals and in the lives of their organizations only in so far as it opened believers to the summons of the gospel. One might say that of itself ministry did not possess authority but that it transferred authority to those being ministered to. Theirs were the decisions, and the decisions became authoritative in so far as they conformed with the gospel. What the minister knew to be the way of the gospel had to become the mind also of the believers.

In this process, as we saw in Paul's handling of the conflict about the authenticity of his ministry, an authoritative exercise of ministry challenges members of a community to work their way to a response on the deepest levels of their experience as Christians. If we wish to think of this as being a consultative process, we need to understand that the consultation is not between the minister and the Corinthians but among the Corinthians themselves as they bring to bear upon the problem put to them by their minister the wisdom which has accrued from their experience of life in a Christian congregation. In chapter 14 of his first letter Paul encouraged them to recognize how resourceful prophets can be for such purposes in stimulating everyone— or so it would seem—to 'weigh what is said' (verse 29); certainly, anyone with the prophetic spirit is to contribute to the community's need at such a time. In *The Spirit and the Congregation: Studies in 1 Corinthians 12-15* Ralph P. Martin has written helpfully on this aspect of the prophet's responsibility in the community, showing clearly that Christian order is not the result of 'an imperious call to obedience' but of discerning 'the mind of Christ' (1 Corinthians 2.16). In this sense, the consultation that takes place is as much with Christ in the Spirit as it is with one another, and in its resolution the authority of ministry finds its expression. (Even the extreme case of the incestuous man in chapter 5 of this letter conforms to this pattern; see verse 4: 'When you are assembled, and my spirit is present, with the power of our Lord Jesus, you are to...')

Historical experience of Christian ministries and ministers has not left many of today's Christians with the impression that ultimately the authority of ministry rests with those who are not ministers. How many congregations live by the conviction that the authority of the gospel is their prerogative to give living expression to and that unless the authority of the gospel does reach expression among them the ministry has been ineffective? Rather, is it not the case that when we encounter ministerial titles we too easily assume that the title confers an authority on its holder which he or she is entitled—as we say—to wield within his or her designated field of ministry? That is to say, we assume that ministry confers authority over people. On what we see here, however, in ministry this is not the case.

Interestingly, in our time large sectors of the educated lay members of churches, especially of the churches which operate on a hierarchical model, would heartily concur with this evaluation of the authority of ministry and would gladly accept the responsibilities it requires of congregations; it would appear to correspond with their calls for a church which has a more consultative style, which abdicates absolutist claims inherited from a dubiously Christian participation in the kingdoms of this world, and which at last might open itself to power from below. But in this they would be working on grounds very different from the ground we are working on. For many of these contemporary Christians, ministry must not attempt to display the signs of worldly and coercive power for the reason that the meaning of the *diakon-* words require Christians to make their ministry a service of one another. The instinct leading them to advocate their approach to Christian authority is no doubt sound, and their desire to live in a church where they actually participate in shaping the congregation is authentically Christian, but the part of their brief which is the linguistic argument cannot support them, for, as we have seen, ministry/*diakonia* is not that sort of word at all.

A church will develop a consultative style or display the democratic aspect of the people of God in so far as the ministry reaching it issues in attitudes and actions which the congregation has arrived at in the process of discovering the mind of the Lord; therein the church will also be manifesting the authority of its ministry. We can say this by virtue of what ministry meant for the ancient people who gave us the word. Clearly, if we wish to institute this early Christian perception of an authoritative ministry in our churches, we have much to learn and we have risks to take. The title *minister* does indeed indicate that a person has been charged with a responsibility, but because the responsibilities of Christian ministry are coextensive with—that is, do not exceed—the limits of the gospel, the titled minister has also to learn the limits of ministry's authority.

10: 'Certain which should be chosen'

The term minister/*diakonos*, through which Paul made his most comprehensive claims to apostolic authority, never became a title of those authorized to carry out the ministry of the word in the Christian church. From the point of view of language the reason for this is close to hand. As discussed earlier, the term was useful to Paul because it expressed the connection between what he preached and the heavenly Lord who commissioned him to preach it. It was that sort of word, particularly apt for a person delivering the message of a divinity. In the short time that the word of the gospel took to pass from an original generation to the next, however, the concept of the proclaimer being a minister/*diakonos* had already played itself out because by definition the minister/*diakonos* was under a direct mandate from the divinity. (See the comments above on the case of Epaphras, Colossians 1.7, where the writer has to cope with this requirement.) In a second generation Christian church such a direct mandate was no longer possible, the idea being repugnant to the foundational notion and process of tradition. In recording the reaction of the Lycaonians, devotees of Zeus and Hermes, to the preaching of Paul (Acts 14.11-13), we noted how sedulously Luke avoided applying this designation at any stage even to the original proclaimers, and we suspected that in this he was shielding the tradition from the danger of being eroded through ideas about a mandate for the word of God being delivered to enthusiasts claiming direct illumination from on high.

Ministry and tradition

If the minister/*diakonos* could thus not become a permanent officer for the proclamation of the word, the ministry/*diakonia* itself had to remain as a function if the church was to be church.

In the formula created by the writer of the letter to the Ephesians (4.12), we have seen the ministry/*diakonia* in its rightful place. The value to the church of retaining an awareness of this function is immeasurable, and at any period in the history of the church when the function is appreciated for what it is the church is invigorated. One must instance the enlivening of the word of God at the Reformation. Changes inevitably occur when ministry of the word—ministering the word—passes God's word to the believer, even in the sense of mediating the revelation; the word speaks for itself in the believer, and the role of the ministry is to make it available. If the church is faithful to its charge, the process of ministry is not exposed to perversion at the hands either of mavericks or of magisteriums because in its continuous experience of ministry the church will be living constantly within the tradition that gave it birth. Should a church merely give lip service to tradition, condemning itself to be a prisoner of its past instead of being nourished by the past into new growth and the new shapes of a maturer life, it will begin to live profanely, increasingly putting the form of this world between itself and the source of life and enlightenment. Here the perceptions held by some Orthodox theologians of the *laos*, which is the whole believing people as the guardian of tradition, express a profound insight into the relationship that should exist between tradition and ministry. The ministry gives expression to what the whole church possesses in apostolic tradition.

In this connection we surely see the enriching possibilities of a ministry peopled by those whom the congregations recognize as living and faithful expressions of the tradition. Much Protestant theology of ministry takes its rise from the call of such congregations to an individual, but as experience has shown even this process is not immune to artificiality as well schooled theologians compete for livings among a limited range of desirable opportunities. The meaning of tradition within a congregation requires rather more in the search for a ministry to sustain it than the sittings of a search committee, because the tradition is not the possession of one congregation only but is in the communion of all the congregations.

For this reason the growth and continuance of ministry is the responsibility of all the church, and congregations should give expression to this in sharing responsibility for the vitality of ministry in neighbouring congregations. This communion of responsibility is well represented in the ritual for the ordination of a Roman Catholic bishop when the ordaining bishop is assisted by two or three of his brother bishops. On the other hand, this symbolic representation of tradition at work in the Christian community remains an empty gesture when, as generally in the Roman Catholic Church, the pastors alone organise and shape the ministry. In this church, as suitable ordained personnel become increasingly difficult to obtain in our times, and as the standards of a new orthodoxy impose restrictions on the kind of man deemed eligible for episcopal ordination, we read more and more often of administrative interference in the selection and placement of members of ordained ministry. Of such malaises official ministries die, and time will tell how authentic ministries might be restored. The Roman synod of 1990 on the formation of priests made that time look long.

Deacons new and old

One area of official ministry in the Roman Catholic Church which has sought a reformation is the diaconate. For centuries this ancient section of the church's order had been merely a staging ground of a few months' duration prior to ordination to priesthood. Its antiquity alone seemed to be preserving it, although some remnants of a theological rationale and a few obscure biblical passages were always going to save it from the fate which overtook the so-called minor levels of ecclesiastical order in the aftermath of the Second Vatican Council. The best evidence of its antiquity, of course, is in the title of the deacon himself—we will not go into the area of deaconesses: a compendious resource is available in A. G. Martimort's *Deaconesses: An Historical Study*—for *deacon* is more or less a transliteration of our ancient word *diakonos*/minister. As such the title forms a noteworthy fragment in the history of language. For every other purpose for which ancient Greeks used the *diakon-* words, the Latin language and other languages of Europe translated by whatever terms seemed to suit, very often by *minister* but by no means only this. As applied to the ordained minister, however, something made them keep close to the Greek original with the title *deacon*. This simple fact alone testifies to how deeply embedded in the life of early Christian communities was the idea of special officers set apart by what was soon being called ordination, a ritual consisting of prayer and the laying on of hands.

While historical records such as manuals which enshrine the rites of ordination and memorials to martyrs who were deacons —the outstanding instance here being Laurence of Rome— assure us of the established place of the diaconate in the earlier centuries, its early history is nonetheless obscure and does not require our attention here. What is interesting is that by the time of the Reformation, when its identity and function was for all practical purposes totally lost, leading reformers did not seek to abolish it. Elsie Anne McKee, for example, has detailed the labours of Calvin to rescue the diaconate from its liturgical limbo in Roman Catholicism and re-shape it as a working and official ecclesiastical ministry for the care of the poor. (See *Diakonia in the Classical Reformed Tradition and Today*, which draws on her scholarly enquiry of 1984, *John Calvin on the Diaconate and Liturgical Almsgiving*.)

Luther had less success in this direction and was satisfied if the state took over responsibilities others were entrusting to deacons; nineteenth century Lutherans, however, dedicated themselves strenuously to establishing forms of diaconate which, while not accepted as part of the official ministry, established a large continuing network of institutions and agencies for the assistance of the disadvantaged. A useful summary of this approach to diaconate and of its history is in Jaap van Klinken's *Diakonia: Mutual Helping with Justice and Compassion*. Significant numbers of other denominational churches are continuing today to look for ways of re-introducing or of reforming diaconate.

More or less within the context of these Protestant attempts to re-invigorate diaconate, the movement for a reform or re-constitution of diaconate within the Roman Catholic Church quickly developed during the 1950s in time to gain official recognition in the Second Vatican Council. Given the close historical and sacramental link in this church between diaconate and the celibate ordained priesthood, the achievement of these reformers was remarkable in gaining approval of a diaconate which was to be entered through sacramental ordination, which did not require the deacon to proceed to ordination as a priest and can thus be distinguished as the so-called permanent diaconate, and for which married men could be candidates. While officially the permanent diaconate is said to exist for the threefold purpose of officiating in liturgy, of preaching, and of works of charity, its rationale as put forward in the many training programmes approximates to the Protestant ideal of neighbourly service. Thus, writing for the Bishops' Committee on the Permanent Diaconate in the United States, Timothy J. Shugrue suggests that the two functions of liturgy and preaching should be 'clearly grounded in an immediate and observable form of outreach to those in need', which is the third function, and that the sacramental ordination of the deacon takes place for the purpose of witnessing to this kind of integration of the deacon's roles (*Service Ministry of the Deacon*, p. 62); in such ways the permanent deacon becomes in and for the church 'the image of that Christ ... who leads by serving' (p. 121).

These brief comments on the emergence and style of modern diaconates—in the same vein as the comments in *Diakonia: Re-interpreting the Ancient Sources*—aim to emphasise the intimate connection which all the initiatives assume to exist between the title *diakonos*/deacon and neighbourly service. On this assumption two of the books about deacons just mentioned are called *Diakonia* and a third is called *Service Ministry*, where the word *service* derives in the modern fashion from diakonia. (The title of the third book, *Service Ministry*, exhibits a common but odd coupling of terms because in ecclesiastical language *ministry* also derives from *diakonia*.) In the section called *The servant myth* at the beginning of chapter 7 (pages 86-88) we have once again gone over the development of this modern fashion of equating *diakonia* and *service*, and the reader of this book is well aware of how inadequate and misleading the equation is. But it takes us to the few biblical sources relating to diaconate from which traditionally the idea of the servant deacon has taken its rise.

141

For the reformers of the sixteenth century the significant biblical passage was the story of how the seven Greek men came to be appointed by the apostles—with, we note, the laying on of hands—to 'serve tables' (Acts 6.2). Whatever of the confusion the passage generated among both Protestants and Roman Catholics as to whether these men were ordained deacons—and a vivid tradition of St Stephen the Deacon strongly supported the idea that they were—a consensus existed that their *diakonia* involved assisting the poor by distributing at their tables either food or money. Within our own perspective of *diakonia,* of course, we had no room for either of these understandings, concluding firmly that the *diakonia* of the Seven was no different from that of the Twelve, namely, that it was a *diakonia* or ministry of the word. With the growing scholarly appreciation of the connection of *diakonia* with proclamation, even when the connection is not made on the linguistic grounds that we have been working on, this view will establish itself to the exclusion of the traditional ones which make a connection instead with the idea of service. Currently exemplifying this trend are the comments of Howard C. Kee in *Good News to the Ends of the Earth* (pp.77-78). We thus leave Acts 6 sure that it should not be used as a source for diaconate and that it does not even illustrate the institution of an early form of Christian social service.

That said, no other biblical passage relating to diaconate suggests any connection at all between diaconate and social service. 1 Timothy 3.8-13 sets out requirements of good standing which could be expected of a public figure in any role in the church, while all we have to work from in Philippians 1.1 is that the name *diakonos* occurs in association with that of *episkopos,* the word we translate as *bishop* in 1 Timothy 3.2, where the association recurs. Other early Christian writings, especially the letters of Ignatius of Antioch, and the later church orders which merge into the known history of the diaconate confirm that the association of deacon and bishop is the single most solid element of significant information which we possess about the nature of the diaconate. Reflecting on that association in the light of what we know of the word's usage, we can conclude that the deacon was so called by reason of this association, that is to say, the deacon/*diakonos* was in essence a person who stood in relationship to the bishop/*episkopos* in the same way as the messenger/*diakonos* and the agent/*diakonos* stood in relationship to the source of their authority and identity. The ancients often said that the deacon was the eye and the ear of the bishop; for us to say he was the bishop's right hand man would be to cheapen the currency but would be close to the role. Without a bishop, or at least a superior authority of some kind, like the presbyters in Polycarp, the deacon can have no identity.

In Philippians 1.1, where addressees of the letter include *episkopoi* and *diakonoi*, we can be sure, accordingly, that in the latter we have a case of some lesser officers in the local church whose role was subsidiary to that of some more important officers of the local church, even though in this instance we would be giving a misleading impression of the state of our knowledge of early church order if we called them deacons and bishops. Certainly, from the point of view of language, we cannot take the two words as a two-in-one term for a single group of officials. In saying *officers* here for these Philippian *diakonoi*, however, we do not have to take the impression of a permanent structure already in place, although that could have been the case for this church. On the other hand, both titles could be purely honorific, whether they originated within the Philippian community, as would seem likely, or whether they were applied in the first instance by Paul to some individuals within the community to whom he wished to pay tribute. One other possibility exists, and that is, if the Philippians already had one group of officials whom they called *episkopoi*, Paul could have included in his greetings to them those known to be their assistants whom he designated *diakonoi*; in this case the title would again be honorific, and it could even have stuck. His Greek correspondents were certainly familiar with the use of the word as a minor honorific title for people who involved themselves as waiters in the public sacrificial feasts. In a similar way one would have to think of the word in Paul's address as having a religious connotation. Given the high incidence of religious and even cultic terminology in these pages to the Philippians, one might suspect that both terms are connected with that side of the community's life. From later usage, in

Ignatius and Clement of Rome and then into other literature, the connection of both *episkopos* and *diakonos* with cult or liturgy would seem to be determinative for the significance of these officers in early Christian communities.

Turning briefly from the ancient world back to the present, we can appreciate that our expectations of a contemporary diaconate will vary significantly according to whether we tie it in with *deacon as servant* or with *deacon as the agent of the bishop* (or of some other superior church officer: see the tension this has introduced to Ormonde Plater's treatment in *Many Servants*). In emphasising the connection with service, reformers of the diaconate from the sixteenth century to the late twentieth have sought to re-embody in church order values of service which they have incorrectly attributed to the ancient *diakon-* words. We have now shown that if ideas about and inspiration for a renewed diaconate are to be sought in the past, we would be faithful to the past in exploring the idea of auxiliaries to the bishop or to the ancient bishop's modern equivalent. This not only founds the identity of the deacon in an area other than in service of the needy but opens up to the deacon the whole field of pastoral activity. If the bishop's or pastor's first responsibility is in ministering the word of God, here too is the first area of the deacon's collaboration.

One could build on and on from such a principle. In an age like the present when members of so many congregations are seeking broader representation within the official ministries—as the scores of responses to the Lima document *Baptism, Eucharist, Ministry* testify—here is a way to invite and to develop participation which is in accord with early Christian insight. To suggest as much is not to be wishing a new clericalization upon the denominations or to be recommending the hierarchizing or the catholicizing of ministry; it is rather to be displaying the potential within even our modern society, which is in such need of versatility within ministry, of an ancient ministerial principle. In choosing deacon/*diakonos* as a title for assistants to bishops and presbyters, early Christians were not choosing a lowly term but an honorific and religious term, not however for purposes of aggrandizement in the manner of those 'who are supposed to rule over the

Gentiles' (Mark 10.42) but for the purposes of giving expression to their abiding sense that they were the holy people of God.

Models of ministry?

Discussion about ministry in our time does not proceed far before the model of the ministry of the Son of man is produced, the source as well as the model, as all aver.

> . . . *the Son of man also came not to be served but to serve, and to give his life as a ransom for many.*
>
> Mark 10.45
>
> *I am among you as one who serves.*
>
> Luke 22.27

In each of these sayings the Greek word for *serve* is the verb *diakonein*, the same as occurs throughout our other sources of ministry, and one of the most confusing moves in exploring the relevance of these sayings to a theology of ministry is to equate the *diakonein* in Luke's saying with the *diakonein* in Mark's. Indeed, one has to be careful in making any claims at all on the basis of a similarity of language about the relevance of these sayings to the kind of ministry/*diakonia* we have been examining in the early church. The reason is simple. If I talk of a minister of state I am on one level of language, of a minister of religion I am on another, on another again with ministering to a mind diseased, or with the poet Shelley's 'ministering spirits', and so on. In encountering church ministries in the New Testament, we have found one to be the ministry of proclaiming and revealing the word of God, another to assist in this ministry by liaising between minister and community, another to be the ministry of representing one's community of saints, another to be an assistant to a superior church officer, and so on. Equally disparate in their fields of application are the uses in Mark and Luke, Jesus saying in Luke that he is 'like a waiter' at his supper with the disciples, and in Mark that he is 'serving by giving his life as a ransom'. In neither case is the idea of the service or ministry in which Jesus is involved related to ideas the early Christians were expressing in their talk about ministry in the church.

Much is often imputed to church ministry from the supper scene where the master speaks of serving his disciples: thus is the minister reminded that his title does not invite him to honors but exhorts him to be a servant to his congregation. To moralize in this fashion, however, is to confuse the usages we have just referred to. As a matter of fact, and as we have insisted, ancient usage requires the minister/*diakonos* of the gospel to recognize in his or her title one of the most significant and honourable designations in the religious inventory; it speaks a lot about dignity and authority.

If we are looking for moral values in the service of Jesus at Luke's supper we have to look rather at the values Luke, the Hellenistic writer, would have associated with ministry/*diakonia* at a meal. This takes us back to Athenaeus in the section of chapter 7 above called *At God's table* (pages 102-106) where we considered that for the Greeks the meal was an occasion of communion with the gods and that in giving expression to this conviction they chose not to be served by slaves but by free men; moreover, for the service at table on occasions when they were honoring the religious dimensions of the meal they reserved the term ministry/*diakonia*. We also saw that an ancient, widespread, and revered custom was for masters to attend on their slaves. Such ritualised meals are the context from which Luke took the word for Jesus' service at the supper. The teaching of Jesus is indeed about masters in the Christian community not 'exercising lordship', which is to exult in profane dignity and to employ coercive power, but the teaching acknowledges the presence in the community of great ones and of leaders (verse 26) whose functions in the community are going to be anything but lowly service of their fellow believers. More than with a moral dimension, Luke is concerned with making present the Lord in the food and in mutual exchanges of the community meal.

Virtually all this century scholars have discussed the relationship of this scene in Luke with the scene from which Jesus' saying in Mark comes. While the contexts of the sayings in the two gospels are totally diverse, one being Jesus's last supper and the other being 'on the road, going up to Jerusalem' (Mark 10.32), the climactic moment in Mark's gospel, substantial elements within the scene are the same. Thus what occasions Jesus' teaching is a dispute among the disciples about rank and authority: Jesus contrasts standards of leadership among disciples with the practice of coercive political power, and the teaching for the community of disciples polarizes extremes of social status, one of these polarities being *the servant* (expressed in Mark by the common noun *diakonos* and in Luke by the verb's participle used as a noun, *diakonon*, 'the attending one'). Indications of interdependence between the two gospels at this point could be taken further, but these suffice for us to be sure that a relationship exists.

Of course literary relationships exist throughout the gospels and are often explained through the use of a common source or tradition, while the minor variations which also exist are attributed either to the particular tradition inherited by an evangelist or to the evangelist's own editorial activity. (For example, the temptation of Jesus on the pinnacle of the temple is second of three in Matthew and last of three in Luke, where it makes a suitable climax for a writer with a particular interest in the relationship of Jesus to the temple.) In the instance we are considering what is especially noticeable is the fact that Luke does not contain a statement like that in Mark about the ransoming of Jesus' life. Because this statement is of such great interest from the theological point of view, the question arises, did Luke know of it and omit it or did Mark add it? Before attempting to answer such bald alternatives, scholars prefer to ask a few other questions, one of these being did Luke have an independent tradition of this teaching which did not include the saying about the ransom? If he did, why did he prefer that version to Mark's when most scholars understand that Luke had Mark's gospel to hand as a source and model? These and numerous other questions open up into a wide field of literary theory and of the theological purposes of the two gospel writers.

Now although we do not need to go that way, we are pausing at the questions because in their answers many writers swing a considerable amount of their argumentation around the way they understand the word Mark uses for *to serve*. Since they take a lead from what the dictionaries say about the word, they will be thinking of *diakon-* as a word which basically means *service at table,* and then, since Luke's version of the teaching uses the word precisely in this sense, they will argue that his version is the earlier, and that Mark has changed its setting from a supper to the road on the way up to Jerusalem and has then transformed its meaning by introducing his theology of Jesus's death as a ransom.

Numerous other approaches to the question of the relationship between Mark and Luke at this point could also be cited, many of them similarly assuming that Mark's word for *service* is pointing basically to service of a lowly kind. Even among scholars, but time and again in church documents and in theological and inspirational writing about a series of matters—such matters as the role of ministry, the nature of diaconate, and the Christian responsibility for the disadvantaged, for the environment, and in the politico-economic structures of our world—we often read in all of this that the mandate has been issued and the example provided by the Son of man 'who came to serve'. Almost without exception, in these contexts the writers are thinking of service of one's fellow human being. One popular paraphrase of the bible puts the understanding of service/*diakonia* unequivocally when it says at Mark 10.45 that Jesus came 'to help others'.

When we transfer the values inherent in such an understanding of the service of the Son of man to the ministry/*diakonia* of the ordained or commissioned ministers of the churches, we are quickly back among the questions people ask about why individuals need to be ordained for ministry and why churches do not acknowledge the capacity of all their members for ministry or, if they do acknowledge that all members are ministers—as some do in their revised modern constitutions—why the governing authorities in these churches do not make the administrative and structural changes necessary for implementing a church-wide ministry.

Against this line of thinking about ministry, which sees the Greek words at its base expressing a more or less univocal sense of service, our review in this book has been establishing that in the Greek words for ministry we have a variety of usage where we need to distinguish one usage from another if we are to arrive at a sound evaluation of an ancient statement using these terms. We recall the altogether singular value Paul attached to his title of minister/*diakonos* and the totally different but again singular and significant value he attached to his designation of Phoebe as minister/*diakonos*. Such uses are not univocal, and neither of them designates service of any ordinary kind.

Just as in Paul and elsewhere in the letters and Acts of the New Testament we have identified a variety of ministries all designated by the Greek *diakon-* words, so in the narrative and teaching of the gospels usage varies. The mere presence of a *diakon-* word in a gospel narrative, parable, or teaching does not, however, make the passage significant for the theology of ministry. The passage as a whole has got to have a relevance for ministry before we begin to build it into theology. Each of the first three gospels, for example, contains a statement that certain women followed Jesus and *ministered* to him (Mark 15.41); this statement is to be examined for what it tells us about women in the career of Jesus and for how Mark might relate it to women being the first witnesses of the resurrection, but it has no bearing on the theology or style of ministry in the churches.

Again, in the sayings of Jesus about disciples becoming servants we ought not to leap to conclusions about the nature of ministry in the churches or about its authority. How often do we read or hear a development of the theme that the ministry of the church is not an office of power but a ministry of service? These themes universally invoke the saying 'whoever would be great among you must be your servant' (Mark 10.43) or one of the several sayings like it in parallel places of other gospels and in Mark 9.35, Matthew 23.11, Luke 9.48 and John 12.26. That these teachings are directed against misuse of what we would call ministry's authority is obvious, but that the teachings are directing how what we call ministry is to be carried out is not at all obvious.

We cannot conclude, as numbers pretend to, that the authority of ministry is in the quality of the service it provides, and we cannot make any direct applications of the sayings to the theology or practice of ministry on the grounds simply that the Greek word *diakonos*/minister occurs in the sayings. The only reason the word appears in these sayings is that the writer needed to have a suitable word to designate a person standing at the opposite end of the social scale to the person who stands at the top of the scale. The sayings contrast in these ways the great, the greatest, the first, and the leader with the least, the last, the youngest, the slave, and the servant/*diakonos*, this last being clearly just another in the series. None of the sayings is an instruction about more senior or more authoritative figures in the community taking up menial duties in the community. All of the sayings are teaching that the Kingdom of God does not draw its power and authority from human resources. Thus no one is to seek leadership as an exercise in power, and no one in authority is to think he or she has worldly power. Every disciple, whether the greatest or the youngest, is on the same level as a recipient of the benefits of the kingdom, and in the face of the kingdom every disciple is powerless, like the child in a set of sayings of similar import (Matthew 18.1-4; Mark 9.33-37; Luke 9.46-48).

The word *diakonos* appears in these sayings for the same reason that it occurs in the parable of the sheep and the goats (Matthew 25.44). There, those who have been sentenced to eternal fire for not having given food, drink, shelter, and comfort to people in need ask the king when was it that they did not minister/*diakon-* to him. Many modern Christians read of the ministry/*diakonia* in this phrase as—to cite Jaap van Klinken's book referred to earlier —'a specialised function or office within the church, related to the poor' (p. 30). In other words, they read the word in this parable as if it were the name of the service Christians owe one another. It is not. As the storyteller makes plain, the word is addressed to the king, and by this word his unfortunate characters are naming the kind of service which butlers, valets, and cupbearers owe to the kings and the lords of this earth. Thus, in this story, the word represents none of the values which have brought the righteous their welcome into the heavenly kingdom; on the contrary, it is a sign that the unrighteous continue to think in terms of worldly kingdoms. The author of the Greek version of the parable has used *diakon-* at this juncture because, as non-Christian historians and novelists illustrate, it is the appropriate word for attendance upon the kings and great ones of this world.

With this scene in mind we can return to Mark 10.45, because that saying comes at the end of an episode which begins in the courts of heaven and proceeds in its teaching through the halls of the lords and great ones down to the level at which God's kingdom operates, which is among those who know they have no power of their own, exemplified here by the servant/*diakonos* and the slave of the great houses. Capping the teaching, Mark's Jesus clarifies once and for all that, contrary to the glorious expectations of the sons of Zebedee, his role has nothing to do with the great houses and their entourages—he has not come to be attended upon (*diakon-*) at that level; in a bold switch not unprecedented in teaching attributed to Jesus, he states instead that he has come to attend upon (*diakon-*) the interests of the King-dom of God by giving his life as a ransom for many. The ministry/*diakonia* of the Son of man in this passage is *to carry out his sacred commission*, an idea exactly and, in this context of great houses with their complements of servants, cleverly expressed by the verb *diakonesai*/to serve, to minister.

'The office to preach the atonement'

Asked 'What is the church's mission?' most Christians would be happy to reply, 'To continue the mission of Jesus.' His mission, which is the *diakonia* of Mark 10.45, is also his *ministry*. The church does not lay down its life, but in commemorating his death and resurrection it makes a fellowship in which it recognizes itself as his body in the world. At the heart of fellowship is shared experience of faith. Without the sharing the body does not know it is alive. This brings to mind the upbuilding contributions to fellowship of prophets as sketched in Paul's program for the Corinthians. And the whole process begins in 'the ministry of reconciliation', what William Tyndale wondrously called 'the office to preach the atonement' (2 Corinthians 5.18).

The need to be at one with fellow believers is being felt more keenly in the present years as a response to the heightened awareness of the meaning of being at one with God in Christ. This movement towards reconciliation or atonement (in that word's early sense: Wyclif even spoke of 'onement') leads to many communal experiments. I recall an incident on a visit to Dublin from Melbourne in the late summer of 1990. In the home of a friend I was taken by surprise to see on top of the journals and discarded printouts which spilled over from his study a copy of the journal resolutely founded by another friend of mine. The journal is called *Nelen Yubu*, the strange words being from the Ngankikurungurr language used by people of the Daly River in Australia's north-west. The words mean 'good way', and their significance, according to the editorial note, is that they express the aim of the missiological unit whose work the journal advances. The unit works 'to find the "good way" to walk in obedience to Christ, in continuity with ancestral traditions and in response to the conditions of living in modern technological Australia.'

What interested me was that this gospel journey had been initiated by a philosopher friend bred on Aristotle, Aquinas, and G. E. Moore but who writes in this journal of a conversion from being a Mass-priest—albeit a Vatican II Mass-priest—to being a facilitator of small local groups of Christians on a model of Christianity he had experienced in a Lumko course in Lesotho, South Africa. Conceding that eucharist may well remain 'central', this pastor has discovered the 'basic' Christian activity, and reports it in this way (Martin Wilson, *Nelen Yubu*, no. 43, Winter 1990):

> Lumko proposes gospel-sharing as the basic christian specifically religious activity. One meets Christ there. He is brought right into our homes and neighbourhoods. One meets him frequently. ... When neighbourhood gospel-sharing becomes the basic religious activity, a number of other modern things start to happen. Religion starts to become more involved in everyday life.

The most powerful statement of the rationale for such groups is a short sentence by Gustavo Gutiérrez, one of the makers of liberation theology, from a paper he was to have read at a theological conference in the university of Louvain in 1990 but which he declined to attend because of his duties in a soup kitchen. The paper is entitled, 'How can God be Discussed from the Perspective of Ayacucho?' (*Concilium*, February 1990), and Gutiérrez wrote (p. 112):

> It is impossible to avoid the thrust of the question 'Where is God?' if no answer can be given to the question posed by the Lord 'Where is your brother?'

Over recent decades many Christians of various denominations have been seeking out others with whom they might associate so that, in the course of a growing experience of each other, they could attempt to find the experience of being with the Lord and of having the Lord to guide them. In 1989 I attended a convention in Sydney attended by representatives of some seventy such small groups. My family belongs to one. Our gatherings might number thirty adults and twenty children. We named the group *Oikia*, a Greek word meaning house or household, and we seek to experience being in the household of God.

All through my own church believers are seeking the experience of their common faith in groups of around this size. In the parts of the world from which Gutiérrez speaks, groups form of necessity, to survive as Christians in the ecclesiastical regions called parishes of some tens or scores of thousands of people; among my own middle class contemporaries of the first world we meet of our own choice, not usually on the basis of our neighbourhoods but on the basis of common interests in or perceptions about church: the bonds might be a shared search for prayer, for understanding of bible, for justice and peace, for enriched relationships in marriage or after the failure of marriage... needs which parishes as we have known them cannot have been meeting.

All such groups seek God in the company of their gatherings, and individuals seek it in the group very often because they have no experience of encountering God or their fellow Christians in their institutional worship. The job for ministry is to help people be with their sisters and brothers. People should not have to go looking for them in disparate groups around the suburbs and countryside. The Christian body which is the parish or local church should reveal these relationships and live from them. But it has not succeeded in such a sensitive thing—some will say it cannot—and that is why the call is out for a reform of the structures of ministry. A cathedral is an exhilarating place for a celebration but is not an effective instrument for communication between people. A Corinthian or a Roman house church in Paul's time comprised hardly more than forty people. Working within such a human scale did Paul arrive at his perception of his work as a ministry of reconciliation—that work of arousing forty men and women to live in the belief that they were at one with God—and at his perception of the small gathering as the body of Christ.

Vigorous pastoral measures have indeed been undertaken over the years in very many parishes in an attempt to give some expression to these basic perceptions and to other perceived needs. But parishes remain large, ministers few and decreasing in number, and the bureaucracy required to support the services ever more costly and indeed increasingly impersonal. What small local communities offer in the place of bureaucratized services is mutual knowledge and mutual support; such communities have an inbuilt referral system. The Roman Catholic Church is unfortunately in the process of deciding that the great church will not begin to revivify itself by authorizing the development of such church life. This is the conclusion one must draw from the Roman synod of 1990 on the formation of priests, and judging by the abstract of the postsynodal Apostolic Exhortation (*The Tablet*, 18/25 April 1992) this conclusion would seem to be confirmed. In recommending the continuation of a ministerial priesthood which is exclusively male and celibate, for induction into which a rigorous academic program is required, and in preparation for which a so-called spiritual formation virtually removes candidates from the challenge and testing of life in today's society, the synod has put pastoral renewal beyond the reach of its church.

In the course of formulating a synodal policy of such limited vision for ministry in the church, some participants, including highly placed spokesmen in the Vatican, derided the one strategy which could have led to a new age of church. This was the calling to ordination of men of good standing, the *viri probati* of the church's Latin, whether married or not. The prophetic Bishop Valfredo Tepe of Ilhéus, Brazil, who had promoted this strategy at the synod on the priesthood in 1971 only to see it sidelined by a margin of some twenty votes among some two hundred bishops (as reported in *The Tablet* of London, 13 October 1990) left the following tragic words on record at the synod of 1990: 'There are no human forecasts that in the forthcoming generations there will arise sufficient authentic celibate vocations for pastoral service...' (*L'Osservatore Romano*, Weekly Edition, 8 October 1990).

What is at issue in this is a lack of will (or is it of understanding?) to recognize ministers of the word as authentic builders of Christian churches. It is one thing for a few theologians and some not very well informed activists to issue assurances that any group of Christians has together all the resources among themselves for word and sacrament, but that way lie canonical retributions, breaking of communion, schismatic splintering and atrophy. Nor is it sufficient for pastoral theologians to devise styles of gathering which are priestless. This was the initial recommendation also of the Supreme Pastor in his concluding address to the Roman synod. The purpose would be that, before 'the great threat which some of the sects represent', Roman Catholic faithful might 'draw strength from the hearing of the Word of God, the reception of Holy Communion, prayer and fraternal unity' (*L'Osservatore Romano*, Weekly Edition, 5 November 1990).

In such a program the one Roman Catholic element of a church which is lacking is the leader of eucharist. It would seem, however, that the requirements of the dominant but debatable theology come first. This is the theology which imputes to the leader of eucharist—in a phrase from the same address of John Paul II—'the specific ontology which unites the priesthood to Christ, the High Priest'. As a consequence neither married men nor married or unmarried women will be considered as potential candidates for the ministry which the church needs and which innumerable men and women are suited for. These limitations upon ministry, despite their disastrous implications for pastoral strategy, are increasingly endorsed also in the more conservative type of theology which is attempting to counter what it considers contemporary inroads into traditional theory of priesthood. The same conservative theology will agree that without a minister Christians cannot live fully as church to one another or as church in communion with neighbouring churches, but nonetheless, in being unable to provide a workable principle of ministry for our times, this theology will oversee the passing of hundreds of thousands of believers to the nameless 'sects' whose ministry is versatile and has the capacity to reach people.

These last pages I had envisaged before I began writing this book as a series of chapters on the primacy of the ministry of the word, on the connection between such ministry and eucharist, on the availability of that ministry to women as to men, on the multiplication of that ministry among women and men who might be called forth in the true meaning of ministry so that the body of Christ might be fully represented in more places without the canonical and bureaucratic hindrances to growth which are currently throttling churches, on the building of communion between small churches, on the recognition of ministries between churches... And I have ended with something of the same litany with which my preceding book on ministry ended. Perhaps that is right. A colleague with interests in ministry who was working at the institute where I wrote this suggested that the rest of the theology of ministry might best be left to others.

The best thing this book can contribute to the ministerial condition of the church is, once again, the notion of ministry/*diakonia* itself. After all, addressing the Roman synod on 'The Nature of Priesthood', the Prefect of the Congregation for the Doctrine of the Faith, Cardinal Joseph Ratzinger, said that the first consideration in the question of ministry is 'terminological' (*L'Osservatore Romano*, Weekly Edition, 29 October 1990): what *was* the first ministry? In going over this linguistic ground again, and in deepening the enquiry at significant points, my intention has been to make ministry more intelligible and attractive amid today's pastoral needs. Indeed, I set out to speak within range of those countless men and women of various denominations in many parts of the world who are earnestly—and often angrily— trying to find a living shape for ministry amid crises to whose making they did not contribute. From these women and men, perhaps, will come pressures for reform which churchmen and synods are unwilling or too confused to envisage or implement.

An original objective in undertaking the book has never been out of mind, and if I have not succeeded in that I can imagine differences of opinion, and even some bitterness, obscuring the many positive values inherent in a sensitive perception of ministry as *diakonia*. The objective I refer to is establishing a convincing answer to my overriding question,

Are all Christians ministers?

I have sought to provide an answer to this which is in accord with the notions about ministry entertained by early Christians. The answer, I know, is not in accord with most of the new theology of ministry written in recent years. Ironically, it is in accord with one of the main principles of ministry in my own church, and in numerous other churches in East and West who uphold a hierarchical principle, and it is in accord with what almost all the sixteenth century reformers put forward. This last gives me hope that in considering through these pages the authentic character of ministry as *diakonia* Christians of the main denominations will see greater, perhaps even cogent, reason to honor one another's ministry in the communion of the body of Christ.

The leading Puritan and prominent theologian of the Elizabethan era, Thomas Cartwright, provides what to me is an instructive precedent here. Himself ordained by a bishop, yet convinced that the Presbyterian order was in closer accord with the original ministry, he did not seek re-ordination but ministered as he was, sharing the view which his biographer Pearson ascribes to his more radical contemporary Walter Travers 'that the ministers lawfully made in any true Church ought to be acknowledged as such in any other' (*Thomas Cartwright and Elizabethan Puritanism 1535-1603*, p. 177). Thus could Cartwright compose the words which head this last chapter (from Alexander Mackennal, *Sketches in the Evolution of English Congregationalism*, pp. 25-26):

It is a part of the Discipline of our Saviour Christ that there should be certain which should be chosen out of the rest to preach the gospel, by preaching whereof the Churches are gathered together. Where, therefore, there is no ministry of the Word, there it is plain that there are no visible and apparent Churches.

Conversely, where we have an authenticated ministry of the word, we have churches, and it is in our perception of *diakonia* as precisely that ministry that we have the potential for ecumenically recognizing ministries among the churches. To take more than this from the Puritan estimation of ministry is not my intention; in particular, we would distort the ancient understanding of ministry as *diakonia* of the word if we saw the minister's authority, as so often in Puritan tradition, in his learning and interpretative skills. As we have seen, the minister's authority is the conviction of faith experienced by those who receive the word; the minister's authenticity, on the other hand, is his or her recognition in and by the church, whether that be by episcopal ordination or some other process. In *Ordination and Vocation, Yesterday and Today* H. J. M. Turner has forcefully reminded us of the importance to authentic ministry of selecting fitting candidates, who may not at all be those who feel themselves attracted to ministry (p. 46):

> the Church, knowing that ministers are required in order that it may fulfil its obligations to its own members and to those outside it, proposes ordination to those whom it recognises as actually or potentially endowed with the gifts needed for ministering; these persons, if willing to respond to the call, accept it as constituting their vocation, even though they may feel a certain reluctance, based perhaps on a feeling of unworthiness; finally, ordination gives them grace and authority to exercise their ministry.

If we bear in mind both the role of the whole church in this process, and the limited nature of what we too easily call the authority of ministry but which is better understood as its authenticity, diverse and rewarding exercises lie before churches which would seek a fuller ministry for and from their men and women.

AUTHORS AND WORKS CITED
(except translations of the Bible)

Abbott, T. K., *A Critical and Exegetical Commentary on the Epistles to the Ephesians and to the Colossians*, The International Critical Commentary (New York: Scribners 1905)

Ainslie, James L., *The Doctrines of Ministerial Order in the Reformed Churches of the 16th and 17th Centuries* (Edinburgh: T. and T. Clark 1940)

Baptism, Eucharist and Ministry, Faith and Order Paper No. 111 (Geneva: World Council of Churches 1982)

Barrett, C. K., *A Commentary on the First Epistle to the Corinthians* (New York: Harper and Row 1968)

Barth, Markus, *Ephesians*, The Anchor Bible (Garden City, NY: Doubleday 1974)

Baum, William Cardinal, 'A Message on the Priesthood', in Robert J. Wister, ed., *Priests: Identity and Ministry* (Wilmington: Glazier 1990), pages 149-157

Bayne, Paul, *An Entire Commentary upon the Whole Epistle of St Paul to the Ephesians* (London 1643, repr. Edinburgh: Nichol; London: Nisbet; Dublin: Herbert 1866)

Beyer, H. W., article on *diakonia* in Gerhard Kittel, ed., *Theological Dictionary of the New Testament*, Eng. trans. vol. 2 (Grand Rapids: Eerdmans 1964)

Bilde, Per, *Flavius Josephus between Jerusalem and Rome* (Sheffield: JSOT Press 1988)

Box, G. H., *The Testament of Abraham* (London: Dent 1922)

Bruce, F. F., *The Epistles to the Colossians, to Philemon, and to the Ephesians* (Grand Rapids: Eerdmans 1984)

Bruce, F. F., *The Pauline Circle* (Exeter: Paternoster Press; Grand Rapids: Eerdmans 1985

Calvin, John, *Institutes of the Christian Religion*, Eng. trans. H. Beveridge, 2 vols (London: James Clarke 1962)

Calvin, John, *The Epistles of Paul the Apostle to the Galatians, Ephesians, Philippians and Colossians*, Eng. trans. T. H. L. Parker (Grand Rapids: Eerdmans 1980)

Card, Terence, *Priesthood and Ministry in Crisis* (London: SCM 1988)

Castellucci, Erio, 'L'identità del presbitero in prospettive cristologica ed ecclesiologica', *Seminarium,* new series, 30(1990)92-139

Castro, Emilio, Report of the General Secretary (WCC), *Ecumenical Review* 42 (1990) 337-348

Chocarne, Père, *The Inner Life of the Very Reverend Père Lacordaire, O. P.,* Eng. trans. 8th ed. (London: Washbourne 1901)

Churches respond to BEM, Official responses to the 'Baptism, Eucharist and Ministry' text, vols I-VI, edited by Max Thurian (Geneva: World Council of Churches 1986-1988)

Collins, John N., *Diakonia: Re-interpreting the Ancient Sources* (New York: Oxford University Press 1990)

Conzelmann, H., *1 Corinthians,* Eng. trans. (Philadelphia: Fortress Press 1975)

Curran, Charles E., *The Crisis in Priestly Ministry* (Notre Dame: Fides 1972)

Doohan, Leonard, *The Lay-Centered Church: Theology and Spirituality* (Minneapolis: Winston Press 1984)

Dulles, Avery, 'Models for Ministerial Priesthood', *Origins,* 11 October 1990

Dunn, Patrick J., *Priesthood: A Re-examination of the Roman Catholic Theology of the Presbyterate* (New York: Alba House 1990)

Ellis, E. Earle, *Pauline Theology: Ministry and Society* (Grand Rapids: Eerdmans; Exeter: Paternoster Press 1989)

Forestell, J. T., *As Ministers of Christ: The Christological Dimension of Ministry in the New Testament* (Mahwah, New Jersey: Paulist Press 1991)

Galot, Jean, *Theology of the Priesthood,* Eng. trans. (San Francisco: Ignatius 1985)

Gréshake, Gisbert, *The Meaning of the Christian Priesthood,* Eng. trans. (Westminster, Maryland: Christian Classics 1989)

Gutiérrez, Gustavo, 'How Can God be Discussed from the Perspective of Ayacucho', *Concilium,* (1990/1) 103-114

Harrisville, Roy A., 'Ministry in the New Testament', in Todd Nichol and Marc Kolden, ed., *Called and Ordained* (Minneapolis: Fortress Press 1990)

Hebblethwaite, Peter, 'Synod agrees with pope that celibacy is alive and well', *National Catholic Reporter* (Kansas City), 9 November 1990

Hill, Craig C., *Hellenists and Hebrews: Reappraising Division within the Earliest Church* (Minneapolis: Fortress Press 1992)

Jewett, Robert, 'Paul, Phoebe, and the Spanish Mission', in Jacob Neusner and others, ed., *The Social World of Formative Christianity and Judaism* (Philadelphia: Fortress Press 1988)

John Paul II, Pope, *'Christifideles Laici,* Apostolic Exhortation on the Laity', *Origins,* 9 February 1989

John Paul II, Pope, 'Holy Father's Evaluation of the Synod', *L'Osservatore Romano,* Weekly Edition, 5 November 1990

John Paul II, Pope, 'Priestly Identity and the Need for Priests', 1991 Holy Thursday Letter to Priests, *Origins,* 28 March 1991

John Paul II, Pope, *'Pastores Dabo Vobis',* two-page abstract of 222 page Apostolic Exhortation, *The Tablet,* 18/25 April 1992

Kee, Howard C., *Good News to the Ends of the Earth* (London: SCM; Philadelphia: Trinity 1990)

Kelly, George A., 'The priest and his importance to the Catholic Church', *Homiletic and Pastoral Review,* 90(1990)16-21

Kerkhofs, Jan, *'From Frustration to Liberation? A factual approach to ministries in the church',* in Lucas Grollenberg and others, *Minister? Pastor? Prophet? Grass-roots leadership in the churches,* Eng. trans., (London: SCM 1980)

Klinken, Jaap van, *Diakonia: Mutual Helping with Justice and Compassion* (Grand Rapids: Eerdmans; Kampen: Kok 1989)

Knox, John, *The Early Church and the Coming Great Church* (London: Epworth Press 1957)

Kraemer, Hendrik, *A Theology of the Laity* (London: Lutterworth 1958)

Küng, Hans, *The Church,* Eng. trans. (New York: Sheed and Ward 1967)

Laghi, Pio, Archbishop, 'Archbishop Laghi's report on the state of vocations', *L'Osservatore Romano,* English Weekly Edition, 29 October 1990

Lawler, Michael G., *A Theology of Ministry* (Kansas City: Sheed and Ward 1990)

Lemaire, André, *Les ministères aux origines de l'église* (Paris: Cerf 1971)

Lemaire, André, *Ministry in the Church,* Eng. trans. (London: SCM 1977)

Lightfoot, J. B., *Saint Paul's Epistle to the Philippians* (London: Macmillan 1891)

Lloyd-Jones, D. M., *Christian Unity* (Edinburgh and Carlisle, Pennsylvania: Banner of Truth 1980)

Louw, J. P., *Semantics of New Testament Greek* (Philadelphia: Fortress Press and Scholars Press 1982)

Luther, Martin, 'On the Councils and the Church', 1539, *Luther's Works*, vol. 41, pp. 5-178 (Philadelphia: Fortress Press; St Louis: Concordia Publishing House 1955–)

McBrien, Richard P., *Ministry: A Theological, Pastoral Handbook* (San Francisco: Harper & Row 1987)

Mackay, John A., *God's Order: The Ephesian Letter and This Present Time* (New York: Macmillan 1964)

Mackennal, Alexander, *Sketches in the Evolution of English Congregationalism* (London: Nisbet 1901)

Martimort, Aimé Georges, *Deaconesses: An Historical Study*, Eng. trans. (San Francisco: Ignatius Press 1986)

Martin, Ralph P., *The Spirit and the Congregation: Studies in 1 Corinthians 12-15* (Grand Rapids: Eerdmans 1984)

McCord, H. Richard, 'Lay Ministry: Living Its Questions', *Origins*, 19(1990)757-765

McKee, Elsie Anne, *Diakonia in the Classical Reformed Tradition and Today* (Grand Rapids: Eerdmans 1989)

McKee, Elsie Anne, *John Calvin on the Diaconate and Liturgical Almsgiving* (Geneva: Droz 1984)

Merklein, Helmut, *Das kirchliche Amt nach dem Epheserbrief* (Munich: Koesel-Verlag 1973)

National Federation of Priests' Councils in the United States, 'Priestless Parishes: Priests' Perspective', *Origins*, 30 May 1991

Nichols, Aidan, *Holy Order: The Apostolic Ministry from the New Testament to the Second Vatican Council* (Dublin: Veritas 1990)

Ollrog, Wolf-Henning, *Paulus und seine Mitarbeiter* (Neukirchen-Vluyn: Neukirchener Verlag 1979)

O'Meara, Thomas Franklin, *Theology of Ministry* (New York/Ramsey: Paulist Press 1983)

Osborne, Kenan B., *Priesthood: A History of the Ordained Ministry in the Roman Catholic Church* (New York: Paulist Press 1988)

Parent, Rémi, *A Church of the Baptised: Overcoming the Tension between the Clergy and the Laity*, Eng. trans. (New York: Paulist Press 1989)

Pearson, A. F. Scott, *Thomas Cartwright and Elizabethan Puritanism*

1535-1603 (Cambridge 1935, repr. Gloucester, Mass.: Peter Smith 1966)

Plan of Union, A. Consultation on Church Union (USA) (1970)

Plater, Ormonde, *Many Servants: An Introduction to Deacons* (Cambridge/Boston, Mass.: Cowley Publications 1991)

Rademacher, William, J., *Lay Ministry: A Theological, Spiritual, and Pastoral Handbook* (New York: Crossroad 1991)

Ratzinger, Joseph Cardinal, 'The Nature of Priesthood', *L'Osservatore Romano*, Weekly Edition, 29 October 1990

Schillebeeckx, Edward, *The Church with a Human Face: A New and Expanded Theology of Ministry*, Eng. trans. (London: SCM 1985)

Schlier, Heinrich, *Der Brief an die Epheser* (Dusseldorf: Patmos 1957)

Schweizer, Eduard, *Church Order in the New Testament*, Eng. trans. (London: SCM 1961)

'Second Helvetic Confession, The', in *The Constitution of the United Presbyterian Church in the United States of America*, Part I, *Book of Confessions*, 2d ed. (New York: Office of the General Assembly 1970)

Shugrue, Timothy J., *Service Ministry of the Deacon* (Washington: United States Catholic Conference 1988)

Tepe, Valfredo, Bishop, 'Critical Priest Shortage', *L'Osservatore Romano*, English Weekly Edition, 8 October 1990

Thurston, Bonnie Bowman, *The Widows: A Women's Ministry in the Early Church* (Minneapolis: Fortress Press 1989)

Turner, H. J. M., *Ordination and Vocation, Yesterday and Today* (Worthing and Folkestone: Churchman 1990)

Vatican Report on the Worldwide Redistribution of Priests, *Origins*, 28 March 1991

Weakland, Rembert, Archbishop, 'From Dream to Reality to Vision', *Origins*, 11 October 1990

Weber, Hans-Ruedi, *Living in the Image of Christ* (Geneva: WCC Publications 1986)

Weigle, Luther A., ed., *The New Testament Octapla* (New York: Nelson, c. 1962)

Weiss, J., *Der erste Korintherbrief* (Gottingen: Vandenhoeck and Ruprecht 1910)

Whitehead, James D., and Whitehead, Evelyn Eaton, *The Emerging Laity: Returning Leadership to the Community of Faith* (New York: Doubleday 1986)

Wilson, Martin, 'Church Model: Lumko Vision', *Nelen Yubu* (no. 43, Winter 1990) 3-5

INDEX OF NAMES

INDEX OF NEW TESTAMENT PASSAGES

JOHN E. COCKAYNE, JR.